"In a convincing and documented way, rooted in a mature eucharistic ecclesiology, Paul McPartlan shows in these pages not only the need for a ministry of unity at the universal level in the life of the Church, but also the reality of such a ministry in the divine plan of salvific communion. This beautiful text is both a fruit of Catholic-Orthodox ecumenical dialogue and a clear sign of hope for the future of that dialogue."

MOST REV. BRUNO FORTE,
ARCHBISHOP OF CHIETI-VASTO*

"Clear and well documented, this excellent study provides a highly constructive approach to papal primacy. Pope John Paul II insisted that, when discussing the ministry of the Bishop of Rome in the universal Church, we need to be 'open to a new situation.' Fr. Paul's book enables us to do precisely that. It will be of great help in the ongoing discussions of the international commission for Catholic-Orthodox dialogue."

METROPOLITAN KALLISTOS (WARE) OF DIOKLEIA*

"As a theologian and an expert in ecumenical dialogue with the Orthodox Church, Paul McPartlan is striving to explore paths of convergence on the very challenging issue of papal primacy. In this study, the historical approach and the theological systematic reflection nurture each other. For Catholics, papal primacy, as defined in both Vatican councils, is the stable guarantee of the unity of the Church. One cannot but wish that this book may bring both Churches closer thanks to that 'service of love' as propounded by Prof. McPartlan."

MOST REV. ROLAND MINNERATH,
ARCHBISHOP OF DIJON*

*Member of the Joint International Commission for Theological Dialogue between the Roman Catholic Church and the Orthodox Church

"Paul McPartlan restores the eucharistic perspective to its rightful place in discussion of the relationship between conciliarity and primacy. He convincingly proposes to the Orthodox a papal primacy that is not devoid of content, while arguing that Catholics should retrieve a more conciliar and communal form of Petrine ministry—a ministry of unity, charity and peace, rooted in the Eucharist. Profound and yet succinct, academic yet accessible, McPartlan's book is indispensable for any discussion of the structural implications of eucharistic ecclesiology."

REV. DR. RADU BORDEIANU,
DUQUESNE UNIVERSITY; PRESIDENT, ORTHODOX
THEOLOGICAL SOCIETY OF AMERICA

"Paul McPartlan's book presents the enduring Petrine ministry in a new light, as a ministry grounded in the Eucharist. This is a fresh approach that generates hope for healing the wounds of disunity in the body of Christ. An insightful book with far-reaching practical implications."

LADISLAS ORSY, SJ, PROFESSOR OF LAW,
GEORGETOWN UNIVERSITY

A SERVICE
OF LOVE

CUA
August 2013

To President Garvey,

With best wishes,

Paul McPartlan.

A SERVICE
OF LOVE

Papal Primacy, the Eucharist, and Church Unity

PAUL McPARTLAN

The Catholic University of America Press
Washington, D.C.

Cataloging-in-Publication Data available from
the Library of Congress

CONTENTS

ACKNOWLEDGMENTS

I am very grateful to Msgr. David Manson and Rev. Dr. Peter McGrail, who kindly read this work in draft form and made helpful comments, and also to my former research assistant, Jacob Wood, who did valuable research on the *"per Petrum"* notion for me. I would like also to thank Prof. Ken Pennington for some helpful bibliographical suggestions. This book originated in close connection with my work as a member of the Joint International Commission for Theological Dialogue between the Roman Catholic Church and the Orthodox Church and I gladly and gratefully dedicate it to my colleagues, Catholic and Orthodox, in that dialogue.

Ut unum sint!

ABBREVIATIONS

ACO   E. Schwartz, ed., *Acta Conciliorum Oecumenicorum* (1927–84)

CCC   *Catechism of the Catholic Church* (1997)

CD   Second Vatican Council, Decree on the Pastoral Office of Bishops in the Church, *Christus Dominus* (1965)

CDF   Congregation for the Doctrine of the Faith

CIC   *Codex Iuris Canonici* (*Code of Canon Law,* 1983)

CN   CDF, Letter to the Bishops of the Catholic Church on Some Aspects of the Church Understood as Communion, *Communionis Notio* (1992)

DH   Heinrich Denzinger, *Enchiridion symbolorum definitionum et declarationum de rebus fidei et morum,* edited by Peter Hünermann (Bologna: Edizioni Dehoniane, 2001)

DV   Second Vatican Council, Dogmatic Constitution on Divine Revelation, *Dei Verbum* (1965)

GS   Second Vatican Council, Pastoral Constitution on the Church in the Modern World, *Gaudium et Spes* (1965)

LG   Second Vatican Council, Dogmatic Constitution on the Church, *Lumen Gentium* (1964)

Mansi   G. D. Mansi, ed., *Sacrorum Conciliorum Nova et Amplissima Collectio,* 53 tomes (1759–1927)

MD	Joint International Commission for Theological Dialogue between the Roman Catholic Church and the Orthodox Church, *The Mystery of the Church and of the Eucharist in the Light of the Mystery of the Holy Trinity* (1982; the "Munich document")
MGH	*Monumenta Germaniae Historica*
ND	J. Neuner and J. Dupuis, eds., *The Christian Faith in the Doctrinal Documents of the Catholic Church,* 7th ed. (New York: Alba House, 2001)
OE	Second Vatican Council, Decree on the Catholic Eastern Churches, *Orientalium Ecclesiarum* (1964)
PG	J. P. Migne, ed., *Patrologia Graeca,* 162 vols. (1857–66)
PL	J. P. Migne, ed., *Patrologia Latina,* 221 vols. (1844–64)
RD	Joint International Commission for Theological Dialogue between the Roman Catholic Church and the Orthodox Church, *Ecclesiological and Canonical Consequences of the Sacramental Nature of the Church: Ecclesial Communion, Conciliarity, and Authority* (2007; the "Ravenna document")
SC	Second Vatican Council, Constitution on the Sacred Liturgy, *Sacrosanctum Concilium* (1963)
SCar	Pope Benedict XVI, Apostolic Exhortation, *Sacramentum Caritatis* (2007)
UR	Second Vatican Council, Decree on Ecumenism, *Unitatis Redintegratio* (1964)

INTRODUCTION

The 2007 Ravenna document (hereafter, RD) of the international Catholic-Orthodox theological dialogue was entitled *Ecclesiological and Canonical Consequences of the Sacramental Nature of the Church: Ecclesial Communion, Conciliarity and Authority*.[1] It considered the church's life at three levels, local, regional, and universal, and it significantly affirmed on behalf of both churches that "[p]rimacy at all levels is a practice firmly grounded in the canonical tradition of the Church" (RD 43.1). Just as significantly, however, it also stated:

Primacy and conciliarity are mutually interdependent. That is why primacy at the different levels of the life of the Church, local, regional and universal, must always be considered in the context of conciliarity, and conciliarity likewise in the context of primacy (RD 43).

Throughout this study, all italics in quotations are in the original unless otherwise indicated, and the dates given for popes are the dates of their pontificates.

1. This document, together with the other agreed statements of the Joint International Commission for Theological Dialogue between the Roman Catholic Church and the Orthodox Church, can be found at http://www.vatican.va/roman_curia/pontifical_councils/chrstuni/sub-index/index_orthodox-ch.htm

Let us clarify both terms immediately. With regard to "conciliarity" (or "synodality"), Ormond Rush helpfully comments: "In maintaining the unity of faith, the church learned early in its history that the Spirit was best discerned when individuals were together, in community, in council, in synod, just as the coming of the Spirit at Pentecost was experienced when they were 'all together' [Acts 2:1]."[2] Most broadly, conciliarity refers to the togetherness that is essential to the Christian life. Jesus died so as "to gather into one the dispersed children of God" (John 11:52), and the members of the church, gathered and united in Christ by the power of the Holy Spirit, participate in the life of God, which is one of perfect communion—*communio*, in Latin, or *koinonia*, in Greek—between the Father, the Son, and the Holy Spirit.[3]

Accordingly, as the Ravenna document states: "Conciliarity reflects the Trinitarian mystery and finds therein its ultimate foundation" (RD 5). The "Trinitarian *koinonia*" is "actualized in the faithful as an organic unity of several members each of whom has a charism, a service or a proper ministry, necessary in their variety and diversity for the edification of all in the one ecclesial body of Christ (cf. 1Cor. 12:4–30)" (RD 6). While this *koinonia* is manifested in the celebration of the Eucharist, it is based on Christian baptism: "each member of the Body of Christ,

2. Ormond Rush, *The Eyes of Faith: The Sense of the Faithful and the Church's Reception of Revelation* (Washington, D.C.: The Catholic University of America Press, 2009), 49.

3. Hence, St Paul's final blessing to the people of Corinth: "The grace of the Lord Jesus Christ, the love of God, and the communion [*koinonia*] of the Holy Spirit be with all of you." (2 Cor. 13:13)

by virtue of baptism, has his or her place and proper responsibility in eucharistic *koinonia*" (RD 5). Moreover, "all the faithful (and not just the bishops) are responsible for the faith professed at their Baptism" (RD 7).

Now, Trinitarian *koinonia* is centered on the person of the Father. The Son is begotten of the Father and the Spirit proceeds from the Father.[4] Communion thus has a structure: in the midst of the *many* there is a unifying *one*; and, since the church participates in the trinitarian life of God, it too has this structure at all levels of its life. The "one" can variously be described as the "head" or as the "first"—*protos*, in Greek, *primus* in Latin—hence we can speak of *primacy*. At all levels of the church's life, then, there is conciliarity and there is primacy, and the two go together. The Ravenna document considers the primacy, respectively, of the bishop among his people at the local level (cf. RD 20), of the metropolitan or patriarch among the bishops at the regional level (cf. RD 24–25), and of the bishop of Rome among the patriarchs or "bishops of the major sees" at the universal level.[5] It may be noted, though the Ravenna document

4. The Western idea that the Spirit proceeds from the Father "and from the Son (*filioque*)" in no way alters the understanding that the Father alone is the source, origin and principle of the Spirit, and indeed of the Trinity. The true meaning of the *filioque* is related to what Eastern fathers intended in saying that the Spirit "takes his origin from the Father by or through the Son." "The Father only generates the Son by breathing ... through him the Holy Spirit and the Son is only begotten by the Father insofar as the spiration ... passes through him. The Father is Father of the One Son only by being for him and through him the origin of the Holy Spirit" (Pontifical Council for Promoting Christian Unity, "The Greek and Latin Traditions Regarding the Procession of the Holy Spirit," 1995).

5. RD 41–42; paragraphs 10 and 44 consider all three levels in summary form.

does not explicitly make this point, that since in the economy Christ himself, the Son incarnate, is "head" of the body (Eph. 5:23; Col. 1:18), "firstborn" of many brethren (Rom. 8:29) and indeed "of all creation" (Col. 1:15; cf. 18), holding "first place in everything" (Col. 1:18), the primate always in some sense images Christ among his brethren.

As Rush indicated above, conciliarity has been a feature of the church since earliest times. The Ravenna document indicates why that is so: conciliarity belongs to the church's "deep-seated nature" and is "founded in the will of Christ for his people"(RD 10). Fundamentally based on baptism, which makes all the faithful brothers and sisters in Christ by the power of the Spirit, conciliarity's regular manifestation is the celebration of the Eucharist. The term is particularly associated, however, with bishops and with their gatherings both regionally and universally in *councils* (or synods), which are "the principal way in which communion among bishops is exercised"(RD 9; cf. 5).[6] Nevertheless, the conciliarity of the bishops is always anchored in that of the church as a whole.[7]

Councils were, and are, normally occasioned by con-

6. There is, of course, a scriptural precedent for all such assemblies in the gathering of "the apostles and the elders" for the council of Jerusalem (Acts 15).

7. With regard to the equivalent idea of "collegiality," Joseph Ratzinger emphasizes that it is related to "the fundamental mystery of the 'We' of the three persons in the one God" and also to "the 'We' of the whole Church." Indeed, he says, the brotherliness of the bishops is an "image" of the "brotherliness" of the Church: "ultimately there is collegiality of the bishops when there is brotherliness of the Church; and the collegiality of the bishops fulfils its meaning only if it serves that brotherliness and is actualized in a brotherly spirit." ("The Pastoral Implications of Episcopal Collegiality," *Concilium*, vol. 1, no. 1, 1965, 20–34, here at 26.)

troversies and crises, for instance the councils held in North Africa in Cyprian's time (mid-third century) to deal with the effects of persecution; and the "ecumenical councils" of greater scope held from the fourth century onwards, after the Roman Empire became Christian. As the Ravenna document says: "when serious problems arose affecting the universal communion and concord between Churches—in regard either to the authentic interpretation of the faith, or to ministries and their relationship to the whole Church, or to the common discipline which fidelity to the Gospel requires—recourse was made to Ecumenical Councils." It continues:

These councils were ecumenical not just because they assembled together bishops from all regions and particularly those of the five major sees, Rome, Constantinople, Alexandria, Antioch, and Jerusalem, according to the ancient order (*taxis*). It was also because their solemn doctrinal decisions and their common faith formulations, especially on crucial points, are binding for all the Churches and all the faithful, for all times and all places. This is why the decisions of the Ecumenical Councils remain normative (RD 35).[8]

As the many quotes from the Ravenna document given above clearly show, the relationship between primacy and conciliarity in the church is a topic of great importance for the ecumenical dialogue between the Roman Catholic Church and the Orthodox Church. In particular, the nature and functioning of that relationship at the universal level of the church's life is a focus of intense study and discussion at the present time, having been the

8. See the Appendix for a listing of the ecumenical councils.

occasion of some of the most serious disputes between Christians East and West in the past. The Ravenna document indicates that "the fact of primacy at the universal level is accepted by both West and East"—a remarkable point of agreement already between Catholics and Orthodox—but that, nevertheless, "there are differences of understanding with regard to the manner in which it is to be exercised, and also with regard to its scriptural and theological foundations" (RD 43.2). In a rather subtle formulation, it speaks of the universal level "where those who are first (*protoi*) in the various regions, together with all the bishops, cooperate in that which concerns the totality of the Church" (RD 10). It should also be noted straightaway that it is a moot point whether the universal primate should primarily be understood just in relation to the *protoi* in the various regions or in a more throughgoing way in relation to all the bishops of the church. Orthodox Christians would generally favor the former option and reject the latter.[9] As will be seen below, however, Catholics are firmly committed to the latter option and generally find the former an unfamiliar notion. The Ravenna document phrases its final request rather openly, and simply asks for "the role of the bishop of Rome in the communion of all the Churches to be studied in greater depth" (RD 45).

The present study is written with the conviction that that role of the universal primate must be deter-

9. Cf. Vlassios Phidas, "Papal Primacy and Patriarchal Pentarchy in the Orthodox Tradition," in *The Petrine Ministry: Catholics and Orthodox in Dialogue,* edited by Cardinal Walter Kasper (New York/Mahwah, N.J.: The Newman Press, 2006), 65–82, here at 80.

mined fundamentally by reference to the mystery of the Eucharist, which is celebrated in each local or particular church but is always and everywhere the one Eucharist of the church as a whole. Notably, it was in the Eucharistic context of the Last Supper that Jesus prayed that all his followers might be one—*Ut unum sint* (John 17:21)—and those words were taken by Pope John Paul II as the title for the encyclical letter in which he famously invited ecumenical discussion of the primacy of the bishop of Rome so that a way of exercising that primacy might be found which "while in no way renouncing what is essential to its mission, is nonetheless open to a new situation."[10] First and foremost, he sought dialogue between the pastors and theologians of the Catholic and Orthodox Churches, "that we may seek—together of course—the forms in which this ministry may accomplish a service of love recognized by all concerned."[11] As its title indicates, the present work hopes to make a contribution to that search.

The Eucharist, in which the faithful regularly receive Holy Communion, lies at the heart of an ecclesiology of communion. Within the Catholic Church, it is recognized that: "[t]he concept of *communion (koinonia)* ... is very suitable for expressing the core of the mystery of the Church, and can certainly be a key for the renew-

10. Pope John Paul II, Encyclical Letter, *Ut Unum Sint* (1995), n. 95.

11. *Ut Unum Sint*, n.95; these words were quoted from a homily of Pope John Paul II in St Peter's Basilica in the presence of Ecumenical Patriarch Dimitrios on December 6, 1987. In *Ut Unum Sint*, Pope John Paul urged again that "the Church must breathe with her two lungs!" and stressed that "the full communion to be sought [between the Church in the East and the Church in the West] is that of unity in legitimate diversity" (n. 54).

al of Catholic ecclesiology"[12] and indeed that the ecclesiology of communion is "the central and fundamental idea" in the documents of Vatican II.[13] Pope Benedict XVI has reiterated the words of his predecessor, Pope John Paul II, that "[t]he Church draws her life from the Eucharist"[14] and added that with regard to the "striking interplay" between the formulae, the Eucharist makes the church and the church makes the Eucharist "the primary causality is expressed in the first formula" (SCar 14). Of particular significance for the present topic is the following statement of Pope Benedict:

The unity of ecclesial communion is concretely manifested in the Christian communities and is renewed in the celebration of the Eucharist, which unites them and differentiates them in the particular Churches "*in quibus et ex quibus una et unica Ecclesia catholica exsistit.*" The fact that the one Eucharist is celebrated in each diocese around its own Bishop helps us to see how those particular Churches subsist [*exsistant*] in and *ex Ecclesia.*[15]

Pope Benedict further emphasizes that the Eucharist "objectively creates a powerful bond of unity between the Catholic Church and the Orthodox Churches, which have preserved the authentic and integral nature

12. Congregation for the Doctrine of the Faith (CDF), Letter to the Bishops of the Catholic Church on Some Aspects of the Church understood as Communion, *Communionis Notio*, 1992 (hereafter, CN), 1.

13. Extraordinary Assembly of the Synod of Bishops (1985), *Final Relatio* II, C, 1.

14. Pope Benedict XVI, Apostolic Exhortation, *Sacramentum Caritatis*, 2007 (hereafter, SCar), 14; cf. Pope John Paul, Encyclical Letter, *Ecclesia de Eucharistia*, 2003, 1.

15. SCar 15; including a quote from Vatican II, *Lumen Gentium* 23.

of the eucharistic mystery" (SCar 15). In their official theological dialogue at the international level, Catholics and Orthodox have already given extensive consideration to the relationship between the church and the Eucharist in the Munich document, *The Mystery of the Church and of the Eucharist in the Light of the Mystery of the Holy Trinity* (1982), and, as seen above, have begun to reflect on the deeply related issue of primacy and conciliarity in the Ravenna document.

Though it mentioned the Eucharist a number of times in connection with the life of the church at the local, regional, and universal levels (cf. RD 3, 5, 6, 11, 12, 15, 18, 23, 26, 33, 34), the Ravenna document did not specifically reflect on the relationship between primacy and conciliarity in the light of the Eucharist. It indicated, however, a desire to move in that direction, by saying the following:

Since the Eucharist, in the light of the Trinitarian mystery, constitutes the criterion of ecclesial life as a whole, how do institutional structures visibly reflect the mystery of this *koinonia*? Since the one and holy Church is realized both in each local Church celebrating the Eucharist and at the same time in the *koinonia* of all the Churches, how does the life of the Churches manifest this sacramental structure? (n.3).

This statement echoes a programmatic statement made in the Munich document:

[T]he church finds its model, its origin and its purpose in the mystery of God, one in three persons. Further still, the eucharist thus understood in the light of the Trinitarian mystery is the criterion for functioning of the life of the Church as a whole. The institutional elements should be nothing but a visible reflection of the reality of the mystery.[16]

It is therefore profoundly in harmony with the dynamic of the international Catholic-Orthodox dialogue since its inception to seek to understand ecclesial structures, and in particular the vital structural issue of the relationship between primacy and conciliarity, in a Eucharistic light. For the purposes of the present study, it is highly significant that the Catholic Church, which especially in medieval times approached this issue primarily from a juridical point of view, has in recent times increasingly adopted a communion/Eucharistic ecclesiology and shown a tendency to view structural questions, and even papal primacy, in this light:

In Christian usage, the word "church" designates the liturgical assembly, but also the local community or the whole universal community of believers. These three meanings are inseparable. "The Church" is the People that God gathers in the whole world. She exists in local communities and is made real as a liturgical, above all a Eucharistic, assembly. She draws her life from the word and the Body of Christ and so herself becomes Christ's Body.[17]

The whole Church is united with the offering and intercession of Christ. Since he has the ministry of Peter in the Church,

16. Munich document, II, 1. Cf. III, 2: "Since Christ is one for the many, [so also] in the church which is his body, the one and the many, the universal and local are necessarily simultaneous.... The one and unique church finds her identity in the *koinonia* of the churches. Unity and multiplicity appear so linked that one could not exist without the other. It is this relationship constitutive of the church that institutions make visible and, so to speak, 'historicize.'"

17. *Catechism of the Catholic Church*, 1997 (hereafter, CCC), 752. Cf.

the Pope is associated with every celebration of the Eucharist, wherein he is named as the sign and servant of the unity of the universal Church (CCC 1369).

This study will make particular reference to the teaching of the Second Vatican Council[18] and to the Eucharistic ecclesiology which, while developing in Orthodox theology,[19] also developed in Catholic theology[20]

CCC, 738: "[I]n her whole being and in all her members, the Church is sent to announce, bear witness, make present, and spread the mystery of the communion of the Holy Trinity." See also Joseph Ratzinger, "the Church lives in eucharistic communities," "[i]ts worship is its constitution." ("The Ecclesiology of the Second Vatican Council," in *Church, Ecumenism and Politics* [Slough: St Paul Publications, 1988], 8.)

18. Unless otherwise indicated, quotations from Vatican II documents are taken from Austin Flannery, ed., *Vatican Council II: The Conciliar and Post Conciliar Documents*, new revised edition (Northport, N.Y./Dublin: Costello Publishing Company/Dominican Publications, 1996), and the following documents are indicated by the abbreviations shown: *Sacrosanctum Concilium* (1963; SC), *Lumen Gentium* (1964; LG), *Orientalium Ecclesiarum* (1964; OE), *Unitatis Redintegratio* (1964; UR), *Christus Dominus* (1965; CD), *Dei Verbum* (1965; DV), *Gaudium et Spes* (1965; GS).

19. See especially, N. Afanassieff, "Una Sancta," *Irenikon* 36 (1963), 436–75 [Nicolas Afanasiev, "Una Sancta," in Michael Plekon, ed., *Tradition Alive* (Lanham, Md.: Rowman and Littlefield, 2003), 3–30]. Also several works by John D. Zizioulas: *Being as Communion: Studies in Personhood and the Church* (London: Darton, Longman and Todd, 1985), esp. chapter 4, "Eucharist and Catholicity," 143–69; *Eucharist, Bishop, Church: The Unity of the Church in the Divine Eucharist and in the Bishop during the First Three Centuries*, translated by Elizabeth Theokritoff (Brookline, Mass.: Holy Cross Orthodox Press, 2001); *Communion and Otherness: Further Studies in Personhood and the Church*, edited by Paul McPartlan (London: T & T Clark, 2006), esp. chapter 8, "The Church as the 'Mystical' Body of Christ," 286–307; *The Eucharistic Communion and the World*, edited by Luke Ben Tallon (London: T & T Clark, 2011).

20. See several works by Henri de Lubac: *Catholicisme* (Paris: Cerf, 1938) [*Catholicism*, translated by Lancelot C. Sheppard and Sister Elizabeth Englund, OCD (San Francisco: Ignatius Press, 1988)]; *Corpus Mysticum: L'eucharistie et L'Église au moyen age*, 2nd ed. (Paris: Aubier 1949) [*Corpus Mysticum: The Eucharist and the Church in the Middle Ages*, translated by Gemma Simmonds, CJ, with Richard Price (London: SCM, 2006)]; *Méditation sur l'Église*, 2nd ed. (Paris: Aubier, 1953) [*The Splendor of the Church*, translated by Michael Mason (San Francisco: Ignatius Press, 1986)]; also,

and doctrine in the twentieth century,[21] and it will seek, from a Catholic point of view, to give a theological and ecclesiological account of the relationship between primacy and conciliarity (or collegiality), drawing also on historical data from the first and second millennia, so as to develop a proposal for an understanding of universal primacy that may be agreeable to both Catholics and Orthodox. There are three chapters, dealing respectively with "Primacy, Collegiality, and Eucharist," "The Second Millennium," and "The First Millennium and the Future." The latter chapter details the proposal being made. It highlights for consideration by both Catholics

Joseph Ratzinger, *Zur Gemeinschaft gerufen: Kirche heute verstehen*, 2nd ed. (Freiburg im Breisgau: Herder, 1991) [*Called to Communion: Understanding the Church Today*, translated by Adrian Walker (San Francisco: Ignatius Press, 1996)]; J. M. R. Tillard, *Chair de l'Église, chair du Christ: Aux sources de l'ecclésiologie de communion* (Paris: Cerf, 1992) [*Flesh of the Church, Flesh of Christ: At the Source of the Ecclesiology of Communion*, translated by Madeleine Beaumont (Collegeville Minn.: Liturgical Press, 2001)]; Walter Cardinal Kasper, *Sakrament der Einheit. Eucharistie und Kirche* (Freiburg: Herder, 2004) [*Sacrament of Unity: The Eucharist and the Church*, translated by Brian McNeil (New York: Crossroad, 2004)]; and several works by Paul McPartlan, "Eucharistic Ecclesiology," *One in Christ* 22 (1986): 314–31; *The Eucharist Makes the Church: Henri de Lubac and John Zizioulas in Dialogue*, 2nd ed. (Fairfax, Va.: Eastern Christian Publications, 2006); *Sacrament of Salvation: An Introduction to Eucharistic Ecclesiology* (Edinburgh: T & T Clark, 1995); "*Ressourcement*, Vatican II, and Eucharistic Ecclesiology," in Gabriel Flynn and Paul D. Murray, eds., Ressourcement: *A Movement for Renewal in Twentieth-Century Catholic Theology* (Oxford: Oxford University Press, 2012), 392–404.

21. It is notable that while Pope Pius XII gave relatively little emphasis to the bond between the Eucharist and the Church in his encyclical letter, *Mystici Corporis* (1943; see nn. 81–84), Pope John Paul began his 2003 encyclical letter, *Ecclesia de Eucharistia*, with the words: "The Church draws her life from the Eucharist" (n. 1). The fact that the latter encyclical letter takes its name from these opening words gives them even greater prominence.

and Orthodox three particular roles for a universal primate which might possibly form the basis for a consensus between us, namely: moderating disputes, presiding at ecumenical councils, and serving Eucharistic communion. Eucharistic ecclesiology is already established as a bond of prime importance between Catholics and Orthodox and as the framework for our future progress toward reconciliation. By means of historical and theological investigation, this study aims to pursue some of the *structural implications* of that ecclesiology.

1

PRIMACY, COLLEGIALITY, AND EUCHARIST

From early Christian times, the bishop presided at the Eucharist in each local church. St Ignatius of Antioch (martyred c.107) understood the bishop as imaging Christ in that role: "wherever the bishop is, there let all his people be; just as wherever Jesus Christ is, there is the catholic church."[1] The *Apostolic Tradition*, a work originating probably in the early third century, likewise gave a Christological understanding of the bishop, who presided over his church and over its Eucharistic celebration, but it showed a development in understanding the bishop also as priestly and apostolic: "now pour forth that power which is from you, of the spirit of leadership that you gave to your beloved Son Jesus Christ, which he gave to the holy apostles, who established the church in every place." "[Bestow,] Father, on this your servant, whom you have chosen for the episcopate, to feed your holy flock and to exercise the high priesthood for you without blame."[2] With reference to both of these patristic

---

1. Ignatius, *Letter to the Smyrnaeans*, 8.
2. *The Apostolic Tradition*, edited by Paul F. Bradshaw, Maxwell E. Johnson, L. Edward Phillips (Minneapolis: Fortress, 2002), 3:3–4 (p. 30).

sources, Vatican II defined that "the fullness of the sacrament of orders," namely the "high priesthood," is conferred by episcopal consecration (LG 21) and that "the principal manifestation of the Church" consists in the gathering of the members of the local church around the bishop for the celebration of the Eucharist, together with his presbyterium and ministers (SC 41, cf. LG 26).

It was immediately after the priestly and Eucharistic definition of the bishop in LG 21 that the council gave its teaching on episcopal collegiality in LG 22: "The order of bishops is the successor of the college of the apostles in their role as teachers and pastors, and in it the apostolic college is perpetuated. Together with their head, the Supreme Pontiff, and never apart from him, they have supreme and full authority over the universal Church" (LG 22). The proximity of these decisive doctrines of Vatican II shows that collegiality is intimately related to the Eucharistic presidency of the bishops.

The council's teaching on collegiality in LG 22–23 was given with many references to St Cyprian, whose teaching on "One Church throughout the world divided into many members" was explicitly quoted (LG 23, note 32). The full passage in Cyprian states: "there is but one Church founded by Christ but it is divided into many members throughout the world; likewise, there is but one episcopate but it is spread amongst the harmonious host of all the numerous bishops."[3] This passage closely resembles Cyprian's teaching in his treatise, *De unitate*

3. Cyprian, *Ep.* 55.24.2; cf. *The Letters of Cyprian of Carthage*, translated by G. W. Clarke, vol.3 (New York/Mahwah, N.J.: Newman Press, 1986), 48.

ecclesiae catholicae: "*episcopatus unus est, cuius a singulis in solidum pars tenetur* [the episcopate is one, a part of which is held by each (bishop) jointly (with the others)]."[4] Henri de Lubac cited the latter phrase (together with a quote from Ignatius of Antioch) when, in 1953, he anticipated the teaching of Vatican II on collegiality and gave a *Eucharistic* explanation of the doctrine:

Each bishop constitutes the unity of his flock, "the people adhering to its priest, cohering with the heavenly sacraments." But each bishop is himself "at peace and in communion" with his brother bishops *who offer the same and unique sacrifice in other places*, and make mention of him in their prayer as he makes mention of all of them in his. He and they together form one episcopate only, and all are alike "at peace and in communion" with the Bishop of Rome, who is Peter's successor and the visible bond of unity; and through them, all the faithful are united.[5]

Here, not only the role of the bishops, but also that of the pope, the bishop of Rome, is described *Eucharistically*. De Lubac followed up this approach when he later argued that the foundational role given by Jesus to Peter

4. Cyprian, *De unitate ecclesiae catholicae*, 5.

5. De Lubac, *The Splendor of the Church*, translated by Michael Mason (San Francisco: Ignatius Press, 1986), 150–51 (orig., 1953; emphasis added). Cyprian wrote: "No doubt the others were all that Peter was, but a primacy is given to Peter, and it is [thus] made clear that there is but one Church and one Chair" (*De unitate* 4, Primacy Text; cf. *St Cyprian: The Lapsed; The Unity of the Catholic Church*, translated by Maurice Bévenot [New York / Mahwah, N.J.: The Newman Press, 1956], 46). He believed that each bishop succeeded all the apostles, including Peter. Peter's chair was thus to be found in every see, but especially in Rome: those who came to Rome came "to the chair of Peter, to the primordial church [*principalem Ecclesiam*], the very source of episcopal unity" (*Ep.* 59.14.1; cf. *The Letters of Cyprian of Carthage*, vol.3, 82).

was transmittable because, at least in Luke's gospel, it was given "within the framework of the Eucharist," that is, "within the framework of what Jesus wishes to see endure until his return."[6] Thus understood, the universal primacy given to Peter continues in the church precisely as a service to the mystery of the Eucharist and to the communion life of the church that derives from the Eucharist.[7] De Lubac then referred to Matthew's gospel, in which: "it is not so much that Peter is raised by some distinctive power above the rest of the Twelve, but rather that he personally received the same power that will be given jointly to the Twelve (himself included, therefore). . . . Peter, in this regard, does not appear as a super-apostle but as the apostle in whom, personally, all that is shared or possessed in common by the entire apostolic college is brought together."[8] De Lubac here presents Peter as what might be called a "corporate personality" in whom is concentrated that which is given to the Twelve as a whole.[9]

Vatican II referred to the same combination of passages in Matthew's gospel:

6. Henri de Lubac, *The Motherhood of the Church* (San Francisco: Ignatius Press, 1982), 287, quoting Jean-Jacques von Allmen, "L'Eglise locale parmi les autres églises locales," *Irenikon* 43 (1970), 512–37, here at 532; cf. Luke 22.

7. Cf. the statement by J. M. R. Tillard: "The Church is made by Eucharist and baptism, not by the papacy. The purpose of the papacy is to give the Eucharist its full dimensions" (*The Bishop of Rome*, translated by John de Satgé [London: SPCK, 1983], 189).

8. De Lubac, *The Motherhood of the Church*, 320, quoting Louis Bouyer, *L'Église de Dieu* (Paris: Cerf, 1970), 463; cf. 473.

9. In this light, it may also be noted that, as Peter is described in Matt. 16:18 as a rock, so all the Twelve are identified as foundation stones of the heavenly Jerusalem in Rev. 21:14.

The Lord made Peter alone the rock-foundation and the holder of the keys of the Church (cf. Matt. 16:18–19), and constituted him shepherd of his whole flock (cf. John 21:15ff.). It is clear, however, that the office of binding and loosing which was given to Peter (Matt. 16:19), was also assigned to the college of the apostles united to its head (Matt. 18:18; 28:16–20) (LG 22).

Yves Congar notes that such scriptural parallels were much highlighted by Pope Innocent III (1198–1216) to justify the singular position of Peter among the Twelve: he regularly receives first what is subsequently given to the Twelve including himself.[10] Pope Innocent and many others in the second millennium tended to add, however, that what was given to the Twelve was given *through Peter* (*per Petrum*), and therefore that the authority of bishops was simply a share in the pope's own authority. Vatican II actually rejected that interpretation as we shall see below, and inclined more toward the corporate interpretation of de Lubac. For instance, the council taught that while the pope himself is "vicar of Christ" (cf. LG 22), all of the bishops are to be understood as "vicars and legates of Christ (LG 27); "in a resplendent and visible manner, [they] take the place of Christ himself, teacher, shepherd and priest, and act in his person [*in Eius persona*]" (LG 21, amended trans.), especially in the celebration of the Eucharist (cf. SC 41, above). It may be said, therefore, that the council speaks not just of Peter but also of the pope in terms compatible with the idea of corporate personality: concentrated in the person of the pope is that which is given to the body of bishops as a whole.

10. Yves Congar, *Église et Papauté* (Paris: Cerf, 1994), 22.

Statements about the role of Peter among the apostles readily translate into statements about the role of the pope among the bishops, since in Catholic understanding the pope is Peter's successor in the midst of the college of bishops which succeeds the college of the apostles. The pope is both a member of the college and its head.

Just as, in accordance with the Lord's decree, St Peter and the rest of the apostles constitute a unique apostolic college, so in like fashion the Roman Pontiff, Peter's successor, and the bishops, the successors of the apostles, are related with and united to one another.... The order of bishops is the successor of the college of the apostles in their role as teachers and pastors, and in it the apostolic college is perpetuated. Together with their head, the Supreme Pontiff, and never apart from him, they have supreme and full authority over the universal Church (LG 22).

Notable here is the indication that the doctrine of collegiality means that the care exercised by each bishop extends from his own local church to the church as a whole. In other words, each bishop cares not just for his own flock, but has a share in the care of the church as a whole.[11] As members of this college, "the bishops, whilst loyally respecting the primacy and pre-eminence of their head, exercise their own proper authority for the good of their faithful, *indeed even for the good of the*

11. Cf. MD, III, 4: "Because the one and only church is made present in his local church, each bishop cannot separate the care for his own church from that of the universal church. When, by the sacrament of ordination, he receives the charism of the Spirit for the *episkope* of one local church, his own, by that very fact he receives the charism of the Spirit for the *episkope* of the entire church."

whole Church, the organic structure and harmony of which are strengthened by the continued influence of the Holy Spirit" (LG 22; emphasis added). This teaching goes beyond that of Vatican I in which it appears that, while each bishop cares for his own flock, it is the pope alone who cares for the whole flock.[12] It fully concurs with the Eucharistic approach to the episcopate and with the teaching of Cyprian noted above: each bishop's care for his local church which celebrates the Eucharist necessarily extends into care for the whole church which celebrates the same Eucharist, since the Eucharist of its nature is the celebration of the church as a whole; and each bishop correspondingly participates in the common episcopal solicitude for the church as a whole.

If such is the common task of the bishops and the pope personifies the college, as indicated above, it is natural to refer to the pope as having, personally, a *solicitude for all the churches*. This expression, originally used by St Paul to refer to his own ministry (cf. 2 Cor. 11:28), was repeatedly used by popes in the early church, for example Siricius in the fourth century, and Innocent I and Leo I in the fifth century. Such an understanding of the pope as embodying the college of bishops is likewise reflected in the statement of Gregory I when he refused the title, *universalis papa*, that would detract from the proper honor of his fellow bishops, and said: "My honour is the honour of the whole Church. My honour is the firm

12. Cf. Vatican I, *Pastor Aeternus* (1870), ch. 3; in Heinrich Denzinger, *Enchiridion symbolorum definitionum et declarationum de rebus fidei et morum*, edited by Peter Hünermann (Bologna: Edizioni Dehoniane, 2001), 3060–61 (hereafter DH).

strength [*solidus vigor*] of my brothers. I am truly honoured when due honour is paid to each and every one."[13]

The tendency since Vatican II to understand the papacy itself Eucharistically[14] has been consistent with the Eucharistic approach to the episcopate that opened the door to the doctrine of collegiality at Vatican II.[15] In line with Vatican II's profoundly Eucharistic approach to the episcopacy, the CDF has stated: "Christ instituted the Eucharist and the episcopate as essentially interlinked realities" (CN 14), and further that the one Eucharist celebrated in many local or particular churches "renders all self-sufficiency on the part of the particular Churches impossible" (CN 11). Local Eucharistic churches are therefore essentially open to one another and the bishops who celebrate the Eucharist in them are essentially in communion with one another. It is Catholic belief that the Lord himself provided for this unity by establishing a specific ministry that would symbolize and serve it, namely the papacy: "the unity of the episcopate involves the existence of a bishop who is head of the *body or college of bishops*, namely the Roman Pontiff" (CN 12). Thus, it can be said that "the existence of the

13. Pope Gregory I, *Ep. 8*, 30 (PL 77, 933C). The passage was quoted by Vatican I (DH 3061), and is quoted here from J. Neuner and J. Dupuis, eds., *The Christian Faith in the Doctrinal Documents of the Catholic Church*, 7th ed. (New York: Alba House, 2001), 318 (hereafter ND). In the next sentence of his letter to Patriarch Eulogius of Alexandria, Gregory continues: "If your holiness calls me *universalis papa*, you deny to yourself what you attribute to me in a universal sense."

14. Cf. above, pp. 10–11.

15. Cf. Joseph Ratzinger, *Church, Ecumenism and Politics*, translated by Robert Nowell, also Frideswide Sandeman (Slough: St. Paul Publications, 1988), 11.

Petrine ministry, which is the foundation of the unity of the episcopate and of the universal Church, bears a profound correspondence to the Eucharistic character of the Church" (CN 11), and that "[t]he unity of the Eucharist and the unity of the episcopate *with Peter and under Peter* are not independent roots of the unity of the Church" (CN 14).[16] There is, in fact, a "fundamental *mutual interiority* between universal Church and particular Church," and the ministry of the bishop of Rome is "a necessary expression" of this mutual interiority. That ministry is therefore properly understood as something "*interior* to each particular Church" (CN 13).

The use of phrases such as "with Peter and under Peter" here further emphasizes the point made above that, in Catholic belief, the pope is the successor of Peter and stands among the bishops as Peter among the apostles. While Irenaeus and Augustine gave lists[17] showing the succession of the bishops of Rome from St Peter,[18] the leading theologian of papal primacy in the first millennium, Pope Leo the Great (440–61), understood himself more strongly as *vicar* of Peter, though he never actually used the term. Like his predecessors, Damasus and Siricius, he referred to himself in accordance with Roman law as "heir" (*haeres*) of Peter, albeit "unworthy" (*indig-*

16. Every valid Eucharist is celebrated in union with the bishop, the pope and the entire church, and either "expresses this universal communion *with Peter* and with the whole Church, or *objectively* calls for it, as in the case of the Christian Churches separated from Rome" (CN 14).

17. Cf. Irenaeus, *Adv. Haer.*, 3, 3, 2–3; Cf. Augustine, *Ep.* 53, 2 (PL 33, 196).

18. Irenaeus starts with Peter and Paul, founders of the church in Rome.

nus),[19] in whose person Peter was present and through whom Peter still taught.[20] The bishops at the council of Chalcedon (451) expressed a similar understanding in their acclamation after Leo's *Tome* was read: "Peter has spoken through Leo."[21] After the council, the bishops said that Leo was "the voice to all of the blessed Peter … imparting the blessedness of his faith to all."[22] A corresponding acclamation was later given at the third Council of Constantinople (681) after the letter of Pope Agatho (678–81) against monothelitism was read by his legates. After that council, the bishops said: "the highest prince of the apostles fought with us: for we had on our side his imitator and the successor in his see … Peter spoke through Agatho [*per Agathonem Petrus loquebatur*]."[23] Leo believed, moreover, that as heir of Peter the bishop of Rome inherited the indivisible unity (*consortium individuae unitatis*) between Peter and Christ.[24] As a result, it was his duty to care for all the churches (cf. 2 Cor. 11:28).[25]

19. Leo, *Serm.* 3, 4 (PL 54, 147A).

20. Cf. Walter Ullmann, "Leo I and the Theme of Papal Primacy," *Journal of Theological Studies* 11 (1960), 25–51, here at 30–35. "Legally, … there is no difference between the heir and the deceased: the latter is literally continued in the former," 34.

21. E. Schwartz, ed., *Acta Conciliorum Oecumenicorum* II, I, pars 2 (1933), 81 [277], n. 23.

22. Leo, *Ep.* 98 (PL 54, 951B), which is actually the letter from Chalcedon to Leo, *Sanctae Synodi Chalcedonensis ad Sanctissimum Papam Romanae Ecclesiae Leonem*.

23. *Prosphoneticus to the Emperor* (Mansi 11: 666C–D). The letter of the council to Pope Agatho, "bishop of the first see of the universal Church," acknowledged that Agatho's letter was "divinely written as by the chief of the apostles [*a summo apostolorum vertice divine perscriptas*]" (Mansi 11: 683C).

24. Leo, *Ep.* 10 (PL 54, 629); cf. *Serm.* 4, 2; 5, 4 (PL 54, 150; 154D). Ullmann points out that *consortium* was another term "taken from the Roman law of inheritance"; "Leo I and the Theme of Papal Primacy," 39, note 2.

25. Cf. Leo, *Ep.* 120, 4. Pope Damasus had already made the connec-

The title, "vicar of Peter," was used by popes up to Innocent III, who adopted the title "vicar of Christ," instead.[26] However, Walter Ullmann considers that Leo's teaching on the *consortium* between Peter and Christ, and on each pope inheriting that unique relationship, "opened the way to the theoretical exposition of Christ's vicariate in the pope" by the medieval canonists and popes.[27] Indeed, he says, "the medieval papacy was built on the juristic foundations laid by Leo."[28] In due course, Innocent III applied to himself the words of Christ: "All authority in heaven and on earth has been given to me" (Matt. 28:18),[29] and, as will be seen below, the idea of the pope having the fullness of power, *plenitudo potestatis*, became firmly established.

Innocent III used the title "vicar of Christ" to indicate his singular *juridical* preeminence over the church. As John A. Watt says, he considered that bishops were "the members of a body of which he was the head," and that they "derived their powers from the head."[30] It was, however, a renewed *Eucharistic* understanding of the church and of the bishop that enabled Vatican II to describe *all bishops* as "vicars of Christ" (cf. LG 27) as seen

tion between the pope's Petrine role as *haeres* and his Pauline *sollicitudo*; Ullmann, "Leo I and the Theme of Papal Primacy," 44.

26. Cf. Eamon Duffy, *Saints and Sinners: A History of the Popes*, 3rd ed. (New Haven & London: Yale University Press, 2006), 128.

27. Ullmann, "Leo I and the Theme of Papal Primacy," 48, n. 2.

28. Ibid., 46.

29. Innocent III, *Serm.* 18 (PL 127, 395C); cited by Ullmann, "Leo I and the Theme of Papal Primacy," 50.

30. John A. Watt, *The Theory of Papal Monarchy in the Thirteenth Century: The Contribution of the Canonists* (London: Burns & Oates, 1965), 85–86.

above.[31] The continuing use of this title by the pope himself (cf. LG 22) now therefore has Eucharistic rather than monarchical overtones; and, as already suggested it has a corporate sense, too,[32] indicating that the pope sums up in his own person the Eucharistic episcopate as a whole.

In Catholic understanding, as seen repeatedly above, the fundamental identity of the pope is that of "bishop of Rome," not archbishop or patriarch; and this title tends to draw attention to his position vis-à-vis the episcopate as a whole, as a bishop among all the bishops, rather than to his standing among the archbishops or patriarchs.[33] The Catholic Church understands his position to be that of Peter among the apostles, but the real key to his particular role among the bishops as a whole may be said to be the Eucharist: he visibly unites all the bishops who celebrate the one mystery which unites all the Christian faithful. The bishops are united in many different regional groupings, and the juridical structures of the church East and West are very different, but that sacramental unity spans all groupings and all structures, and may therefore be said to be the true context of the universal primacy of the pope. It is urgent for Catholics and Orthodox to discern once again the true characteristics of universal primacy aside from administrative and juridical considerations. The Eucharist can guide us in this vital quest.

Summarizing the view of Joseph Ratzinger, Battis-

---

31. Cf. above, p. 19
32. Cf. above, p. 19
33. Cf. above, p. 6

ta Mondin says: "the primacy of the Pope does not relate either to orthodoxy or to orthopraxis but rather to ortho-Eucharist."[34] In his exchange of letters with Metropolitan Damaskinos, Cardinal Ratzinger noted that the legal terminology of "jurisdiction," etc., belongs to the second millennium, and proposed overcoming the obstacle it presents by returning to titles for the pope used in the patristic era: "first in honor" and "president in love." Honor, he said, is "service, obedience to Christ," and the *agape* (love) mentioned in the second title, taken from Ignatius's greeting to the church of Rome, "is in the final analysis a eucharistic concept."

If the Church in the very depth of her being coincides with the Eucharist, then the presidency of love carries with it a responsibility for unity, which has a significance within the Church yet, at the same time, is a responsibility for "distinguishing what is Christian" as against worldly society.... [T]he pope is not an absolute monarch whose will is law, but quite the opposite—he always has to try to resist arbitrary self-will and to call the Church back to the standard of obedience; therefore, however, he must himself be first in obedience.[35]

Patrick J. Burns summarizes the consciousness that Leo had of his office in similar terms: it was "much less

34. Battista Mondin, *Le nuove ecclesiologie* (Roma: Edizioni Paoline, 1980), 171.

35. Joseph Ratzinger, *Pilgrim Fellowship of Faith: The Church as Communion* (San Francisco: Ignatius Press, 2005), 233–34. With regard to the titles "first in honor" and "president in love," he actually said: "I believe that we could correctly define 'jurisdiction over the whole church' on that basis" (233). To be precise, Ignatius of Antioch did not say that the bishop of Rome is "president in love" but that the church of Rome "presides in love." Ignatius, *Letter to the Romans*, Proemium.

an assertion of juridical authority than a confession of ultimate responsibility for peace, unity, and purity of faith in the ecumenical Christian *communio*."[36] As will be seen below, popes repeatedly exercised this responsibility *synodically* in the first millennium. Around the start of the second millennium, however, they increasingly regarded themselves as having a solitary responsibility in a singular position of preeminence.

36. Patrick J. Burns, "Communion, Councils, and Collegiality," in Paul C. Empie and T. Austin Murphy, eds., *Papal Primacy and the Universal Church* (Minneapolis: Augsburg Publishing House, 1974), 151–72, 154.

2

THE SECOND MILLENNIUM

It is no coincidence that the schism between Christian West and East occurred at the same time as the eleventh-century Gregorian reform in the West, named after Pope Gregory VII (1073–85), during which a strongly juridical understanding of the papacy developed. Eamon Duffy considers that "Gregory's was a lonely vision of the papacy. Though he often spoke of other bishops as *confrater or coepiscopus* (brother and fellow bishop) in practice he saw himself fighting a solitary battle, in a world which had turned its back on the demands of the Gospel."[1] It is important to note, however, that the centralization of power in the papacy at this time, increasingly supported by collections of canon law from the late eleventh century onwards, Gratian's *Decretum Gratiani* or *Concordia discordantium canonum* (mid-twelfth century) being the most celebrated, was driven not simply by a will to dominate but rather by the desire to eradicate abuses such as lay investiture and simony, and to assert the freedom and purity of the church.

The result, nevertheless, was a reconfiguration of the

1. Eamon Duffy, *Saints and Sinners: A History of the Popes*, 3rd ed. (New Haven & London: Yale University Press, 2006), 122.

church, "not as a communion of local churches, but as a single international organization, with the Pope at its head."[2] Pictorially speaking, a pyramid, with the pope at the top, replaced a network of local churches, with the local church of Rome, and its bishop, at the center. Under Gregory's like-minded predecessor, Pope Leo IX (1049–54), Cardinal Humbert went to Constantinople in 1054 guided, as Henry Chadwick says, by an "underlying axiom" that "obedience to papal authority was the key to unlock all ... disputed matters."[3] The mutual excommunications between Humbert and Patriarch Michael Cerularius swiftly followed.

Congar refers to the transition in the West at that time from an "ecclesiology of communion" to an "ecclesiology of powers."[4] De Lubac notes that the term "body of Christ" can have three referents: Christ himself, the Eucharist, and the church. The church fathers of the early centuries took for granted the link between the first and the second of these bodies, and concentrated on the link between the second and the third of these bodies ("the Eucharist makes the Church").[5] After Eucharistic controversy in the eleventh century the emphasis changed, however, and the spotlight fell on the link between the first and the second bodies (Christ is really present in the Eucharist by the transubstantiation of the bread and

2. Ibid., 130.

3. Henry Chadwick, *East and West: The Making of a Rift in the Church* (Oxford: Oxford University Press, 2003), 217.

4. Yves Congar, "L' «Ecclesia» ou communauté chrétienne, sujet intégral de l'action liturgique," in J.-P. Jossua and Y. Congar, eds., *La Liturgie après Vatican II* (Paris: Cerf, 1967), 241–82, here at 261.

5. Henri de Lubac, *Corpus Mysticum* (Paris: Aubier, 1949), 104.

wine). The unfortunate result was that the former link between the Eucharist and the church was gradually neglected and forgotten. This fact, he says, "dominates the whole evolution of Eucharistic theories."[6] It may be said that it dominates the whole evolution of ecclesiology also, and explains the "separation of the doctrine of the Eucharist and ecclesiology" that Ratzinger calls "one of the most unfortunate pages of medieval theology."[7]

The medieval scholastics accordingly understood ecclesial office in terms of two powers which they clearly distinguished: power of order, which related to the *Eucharist* and culminated in the priest, and power of jurisdiction over the *church* which the pope possessed fully (*plenitudo potestatis*) and shared with bishops, each of whom he called to share a part of his solicitude (*in partem sollicitudinis*). Congar comments that under Leo IX and Gregory VII, the Church was seen as "a single society subjected to the authority of the pope." "The pope is the universal bishop. The other Churches exist because he calls bishops 'in partem sollicitudinis.'" Canonists and theologians tended to regard the church as "a single diocese, of virtually universal extent, and the pope as the source of every determination of its life."[8]

Two points deserve particular comment: the term "universal bishop" and the paired terms *plenitudo potesta-*

6. Ibid., 288.

7. Joseph Ratzinger, "The Pastoral Implications of Episcopal Collegiality," *Concilium* 1, no.1 (1965), 20–34, here at 28.

8. Y. Congar, "De la communion des églises à une ecclésiologie de l'Église universelle," in Y. Congar and B. D. Dupuy, eds., *L'Épiscopat et l'Église universelle* (Paris: Cerf, 1964), 227–60, here at 238.

tis/in partem sollicitudinis, respectively. First, with regard to the pope as "universal bishop," such an idea tends to imply that each local bishop is simply a vicar of the pope. The title, *"universalis papa,"* which Pope Gregory I had earlier refused,[9] was, however, already used in reference to Pope Hadrian II in the *Libellus satisfactionis* that the papal legates insisted must be read at the start of the Fourth Council of Constantinople (869–70).[10] In many ways, it seems indeed that the different positions of East and West that led to the schism of 1054 were already evident at that council.[11] On one side, as W. de Vries says, there was a tendency by Rome "to make the Roman church alone the decisive judge [*l'instance décisive*] in all matters and thus to leave aside the collegial principle in Church government." In the Byzantine view, however, "the primate did not constitute an essential element in the structure of the Church," and "on occasion he could be left aside and even spurned [*dédaigné*]." The "deepest reason" for the schism that was coming between Rome and Constantinople, he says, "lies in this different understanding of the structure of the Church."[12]

Second, while the terms *plenitudo potestatis* and *in partem sollicitudinis* can already be found in a letter of Pope

9. Cf. above, p. 21.

10. Mansi 16: 28D; cf. W. de Vries, *Orient et Occident: Les structures ecclésiales vues dans l'histoire des sept premiers conciles oecuméniques* (Paris: Cerf, 1974), 263. De Vries notes that in an allocution to the Roman synod in the same year (869), Pope Hadrian declared "that the Roman pontiff has the right to judge all bishops but that he himself cannot be judged by anyone," 263.

11. Cf. below, note 30.

12. De Vries, *Orient et Occident*, 282.

Leo the Great, it must be recalled that he was writing not to a standard bishop of a local church but to his episcopal legate for Illyricum, Bishop Anastasius of Thessalonica, and simply referring to the latter's participation in Leo's power as his personal representative.[13] Moreover, as Robert L. Benson comments, the fact that Leo used the term *plenitudo potestatis* only on that one occasion means that it can hardly be imagined that he intended it to become "the keystone in the theoretical structure of papal power." Nevertheless, as he shows, that is precisely what it had become by the thirteenth century.[14] From the mid-eleventh century onwards, he says, the "publicists and canonists" of the Reform movement "began to improvise more freely with these terms, and to exploit them in their attempts to chart the coordinates of an enlarged papal prerogative."[15] They came to be interpreted as expressing the contrast between the pope's power and that of *every* bishop, with the eventual view that each bishop received a part of the *pope's own* plenitude of power and solicitude.[16]

13. Leo, *Ep.* 14, 1 (PL 54, 671B): "*Vices enim nostras ita tuae credidimus charitati, ut in partem sis vocatus sollicitudinis, non in plenitudinem potestatis.*"

14. Robert L. Benson, "Plenitudo potestatis: Evolution of a formula from Gregory IV to Gratian," *Studia Gratiana* 14 (1967), 193–207, here at 198. Ullmann neglects to mention that Anastasius was Leo's legate (cf. "Leo I and the Theme of Papal Primacy," 36, 45), and his claim, repeatedly citing just the one usage of the phrase, that the pope's *plenitudo potestatis*, as heir of Peter, was already a "Leonine theme" (48, note 2; cf. 40) therefore seems excessive.

15. Benson, "Plenitudo potestatis," 209. See also I. S. Robinson, "Church and Papacy" in J. H. Burns, ed., *The Cambridge History of Medieval Political Thought c.350–c.1450* (Cambridge: Cambridge University Press, 1988), 252–305, especially 266–88.

16. Cf. Jean Rivière, "In partem sollicitudinis: Évolution d'une formule pontificale," *Revue des sciences religieuses* 5 (1925), 210–31, here at 222;

Pope Innocent III "maintained that the jurisdiction of all lesser churches and prelates derives from the Roman See, which has called them 'to a share of its responsibility (*in partem suae sollicitudinis*)' but has retained its own inexhaustible 'fulness of power.'"[17] Already in the late eleventh century, the canonist Bernold of Constance had said: "no bishop has so much power over the flock entrusted to him as does the pope." "Although the pope has divided his own task among individual bishops, nevertheless he has in no way deprived himself of his universal and paramount power, just as a king has not diminished his own royal power, although he has divided his kingdom among various dukes, counts, and judges."[18] As Watt says, "[w]ith Innocent III the term [*plenitudo potestatis*] acquired its final standing: it was he who set the formal seal of official approval on it."[19] The term was fundamentally associated with Innocent's understanding of the pope as "vicar of Christ."[20]

The twelfth century saw the start of a series of general councils (the Lateran councils) to implement re-

also William Henn, "Historical-Theological Synthesis of the Relation between Primacy and Episcopacy during the Second Millennium," in *Il Primato del Successore di Pietro: Atti del simposio teologico. Roma, dicembre 1996* (Città del Vaticano: Libreria Editrice Vaticana, 1998), 222–73; here at 231. Roland Minnerath comments that Leo's phrase, *ut in partem sis vocatus sollicitudinis, non in plenitudinem potestatis* (above, note 13), "deviendra classique dans la doctrine de la primauté au moyen âge"; "La tradition de la primauté pétrinienne au premier millénaire," in *Il Primato del Successore di Pietro*, 117–45; here at 130.

17. Benson, "Plenitudo potestatis," 197.

18. Bernold of Constance, *Apologeticus*, c. 23; quoted by Benson, "Plenitudo potestatis," 212; cf. also Robinson, "Church and Papacy," 278.

19. Watt, *The Theory of Papal Monarchy in the Thirteenth Century*, 85.

20. Ibid., 86–87; cf. above, p. 25.

form, and now these councils, which would come to be regarded as ecumenical in the West, were called by the pope rather than by the emperor. Of particular importance is the fact that, since bishops received their jurisdiction from the pope, episcopal collegiality itself was now understood in a juridical rather than a sacramental way. Episcopacy was no longer part of the sacrament of order, and collegiality came under strong papal influence. General councils, summoned by the pope, were now its normal mode of exercise, and regional councils declined in significance. Many of the functions of synods and councils were taken over by the increasingly internationalized body of cardinals, who met regularly in consistory with the pope. So the pope still acted synodically, but now largely with the cardinals, and episcopal collegiality was eclipsed. Individual bishops became isolated, each as "vicar of the pope," caring just for "a specific portion of the Church."[21] The consistory became "the supreme court of Christendom," and the pope became the "universal ordinary,"[22] the "ordinary judge of all" (*iudex ordinarius singulorum*).[23]

The magnitude of the change from the first millennium is obvious, and against this background the return by Vatican II to an understanding of the *sacramental* basis of episcopal collegiality[24] can be appreciated as truly momentous. Vatican II employed the idea of three

21. Henn, "Historical-Theological Synthesis," 238–39; cf. 227, 252.

22. Duffy, *Saints and Sinners*, 132.

23. Pope Innocent III, *Regestorum sive epistolarum liber secundus*, 277 (PL 214, 843D); cf. Benson, "Plenitudo potestatis," 197.

24. Cf. above, pp. 16–17.

munera, those of teaching, sanctifying and governing (cf. the three offices of Christ as prophet, priest, and king) rather than two *powers* in its teaching on ecclesial ministry. All who are baptized in Christ participate in the three offices (LG 31), but ordained ministers have a particular share in the offices, and that applies first and foremost to the bishops, since they have the fullness of the sacrament of order (LG 21; cf. LG 28 and 29 for presbyters/priests and deacons, respectively). Contrary to scholastic teaching that the power of jurisdiction/government was delegated to bishops by the pope, who thereby shared *his* solicitude with them, the council taught that all three *munera*, including that of governing, are conferred by episcopal ordination (LG 21).[25] It added for good measure that bishops are not to be regarded as "vicars of the Roman Pontiff" (LG 27). This not only restored a sacramental basis for episcopal collegiality, but opened the way to a recognition of the jurisdiction exercised by Eastern Orthodox bishops in their own churches, since the council recognized that there is true apostolic succession and priesthood (and therefore, true sacraments and Eucharist) in the Eastern Churches (UR 15). The Decree on Ecumenism duly stated with great firmness: "To remove all shadow of doubt, . . . this

25. Consequently, whereas Ullmann, writing in 1960 before Vatican II, stressed that a layman could become pope, and that "no sacramental qualities are needed to exercise purely juristic functions of government" ("Leo I and the Theme of Papal Primacy," 51, cf. 28), the 1983 *Code of Canon Law* (CIC), reflecting the teaching of Vatican II, stipulates that, if a newly elected pope is already a bishop, he receives "full and supreme power in the Church" from the moment he accepts his election. If he is not already a bishop, however, "he is immediately to be ordained Bishop" (CIC, can. 332, §1). The clear implication is that papal power, being episcopal, is of sacramental origin.

holy Synod solemnly declares that the Churches of the East ... have the power [*facultatem*] to govern themselves according to their own disciplines, since these are better suited to the character of their faithful and better adapted to foster the good of souls"(UR 16).

In the conciliar deliberations regarding UR 2, which states that "Christ entrusted to the College of the Twelve the task of teaching, ruling, and sanctifying" and that "[a]mong their number he chose Peter," a subtle formulation which indicates that the three offices were given to the Twelve directly and not through Peter, one of the bishops submitted a written *modus* requesting that it be stated that the power of ruling was given "to Peter alone and through Peter [*per Petrum*] to all of the apostles." The formal response, however, stated firmly that the proposal "does not agree with the doctrine of the Constitution *De Ecclesia,* [that is, *Lumen Gentium*, presumably n.21]."[26] This rejection of what we may call the *per Petrum* view at Vatican II is of the utmost significance both historically and theologically. In fact, as William Henn notes, the view that "all jurisdiction flowed from the pope," that is, the *per Petrum* view, was espoused by many Catholic theologians and bishops throughout the second millennium (for example, Aquinas, Torquemada, Cajetan, Bellarmine, Suarez), but was "never finally adopted by the ecumenical councils held in the West during the second millennium," including Vatican I.[27]

26. *Acta Synodalia Sacrosancti Concilii Oecumenici Vaticani II*, vol. III, part 7 (Rome: Typis Polyglottis Vaticanis, 1975), 19.

27. Henn, "Historical-Theological Synthesis," 222–73, 238, cf. also 236–37, 248, 251–52, 266–67. The *per Petrum* idea can already be found in

As just seen, Vatican II was not only consistent with this pattern of conciliar reticence but also conclusive, in that the *per Petrum* view was explicitly set aside.

The *per Petrum* view corresponds to what Henn calls the "new" claim that was made in the eleventh century that the church of Rome is not only "the central, unifying point of reference for the other churches," but rather the "source and origin" of the other churches,[28] such that the latter churches are not only *sisters* of the church of Rome but *daughters*, with Rome being understood as mother and monarch. In two celebrated exchanges between East and West, first Archbishop Nicetas of Nicomedia in debate with Anselm of Havelberg in Constantinople in 1136, and then Patriarch John X Camateros of Constantinople in correspondence with Pope Innocent III in 1198–99 protested that Rome was no longer behaving as a sister. Nicetas recognized that there

---

Leo I: "*In Petro ... omnium fortitudo munitur, et divinae gratiae ita ordinatur auxilium, ut firmitas, quae per Christum Petro tribuitur, per Petrum apostolis conferatur*" (*Serm.* 4, 3; PL 54, 152A); cf. Ullmann, "Leo I and the Theme of Papal Primacy," 45; also, 48. We saw above that Innocent III espoused it also (cf. p. 25, at note 30). In late 1562 and early 1563, a proposed draft canon affirming that bishops called by the Roman Pontiff *in partem sollicitudinis* were true and legitimate prompted a lengthy debate at the Council of Trent on the whole question of the nature and origin of episcopal power (cf. *Concilium Tridentinum Diariorum, Actorum, Epistularum, Tractatuum*, tome 9, 1924, 105–241; the proposed canon 7 is at 107). The final form of the canon, included in the Canons on the Sacrament of Order (1563), simply affirmed, however, that bishops chosen by the authority of the Roman Pontiff (*auctoritate Romani Pontificis*) were true and legitimate (DH 1778). Henn records the sharp division among the bishops attending the council with regard to whether episcopal jurisdiction was conferred by the pope or directly by Christ; "Historical-Theological Synthesis", 250–51. The matter was not resolved until Vatican II.

28. Henn, "Historical-Theological Synthesis," 231.

were "three patriarchal sister sees" in ancient times, namely Rome, Alexandria, and Antioch, among which Rome had received the primacy. "For this reason Rome has been called the first see and it is to her that appeal must be made in doubtful ecclesiastical cases, and it is to her judgement that all matters that cannot be settled according to the normal rules must be submitted." He recalled that the Emperor Phocas (602–10) confirmed, against the claims of Constantinople, based on the latter's role as capital of the Empire, that "the apostolic see of Blessed Peter was the head of all the Churches [*caput omnium Ecclesiarum*]," and Nicetas himself recognized Rome as "holding the highest place [*praesidenti*] in any general council, the first place of honor [*primum honoris locum*]." However, he said, Rome "has appropriated to herself the monarchy which is not contained in her office."[29] John Camateros, in turn, objected: "Where do you find in the holy Gospels that Christ said that the Church of the Romans is the head and universal mother and the most catholic of all the churches ... or by what ecumenical council was what you say about your church decided?" Rome, he contended, was not "mother of the other churches," but rather, among the five patriarchal churches, "first among equal sisters."[30] While there is

29. As recorded by Anselm of Havelberg, *Dialogi*, III, 7–8 (PL 188, 1217D–1218A; 1219A–B); translation slightly amended from Francis Dvornik, *Byzantium and the Roman Primacy* (New York: Fordham University Press, 1966), 145.

30. Quoted by Yves Congar, *Diversity and Communion* (London: SCM, 1984), 87. The idea of Rome as "mother of the Churches" seems to trace back to Pope Nicholas I (858–67), who referred to the church of Rome as "*omnium Ecclesiarum magistra, mater et caput*," Ep.75 (PL 119, 905D); cf. Andrew Louth,

some commonality between these two Eastern voices, Nicetas is distinctive in recognizing genuine prerogatives as pertaining to Rome, because of her "first place of honor," and his words may be helpful for Catholic-Orthodox rapprochement today, particularly in light of the rejection of the *per Petrum* idea by Vatican II.

Even though the three *munera* are all conferred on a new bishop by the sacrament of ordination, Vatican II taught that the *munera* of teaching and ruling "of their very nature can be exercised only in hierarchical communion with the head and members of the college" (LG 21), that is, with the pope and the college of bishops.[31] This stipulation profoundly accords with the fact that since ancient times at least three bishops have been required to confer episcopal ordination on a new bishop,[32] the reason being that, by its nature, episcopal ordination is a collegial act, an act by which the college of bishops receives a new member. Indeed, Vatican II taught that: "One is constituted a member of the episcopal body in

---

Greek East and Latin West: The Church AD 681–1071, The Church in History, vol.3 (Crestwood, N.Y.: St Vladimir's Seminary Press, 2007), 298. Emperor Basil also referred to Rome as "mother of all the Churches" and to the pope as *"universalis papa"* when receiving the papal legates at the Fourth Council of Constantinople; de Vries, *Orient et Occident*, 267.

31. De Vries comments that the Photian dispute (see below, pp. 62–63) already showed a contrast between what would be the Roman view in the second millennium, namely that "the pope confers particular powers on the patriarch which, in the strict sense, pertain to him [the pope] alone" (that is, the *per Petrum* view), and the standard Eastern view, namely that "recognition by all the other patriarchs, and thus also and in first place by Rome" was "necessary for the regular exercise of a function, but not constitutive for the obtaining of that function," *Orient et Occident*, 276. There is a notable similarity between this Eastern view and that of Vatican II.

32. Cf. Council of Nicaea, canon 4; LG 22.

virtue of the sacramental consecration and by the hierarchical communion with the head and members of the college" (LG 22). The *Nota Explicativa Praevia* appended to *Lumen Gentium* further explained that the idea of "communion," which was "highly valued in the early Church" and is valued still today "especially in the East," is "something organic which calls for a juridical structure" (LG, *Nota* 2). The Catholic Church believes that Christ gave such a structure to the church by establishing the college of apostles headed by Peter, and that he intended that structure of unity and leadership to continue in the college of bishops headed by the successor of Peter.[33] This conviction naturally raises a question, however, about the *de facto* exercise of episcopal powers (*potestates*) by Eastern bishops not in communion with the pope and the college of bishops. The council identified this problem but chose not to enter into it (cf. LG, *Nota* 4, the final "N.B.").

The *Nota* also stressed that "there is no such thing as a college without its head," so there can be no action of the bishops without the pope. The bishops are not constituted as a college without the pope, who even in

33. As is well known, the council taught that "the sole Church of Christ ... which our Savior, after his resurrection, entrusted to Peter's pastoral care (John 21:17), commissioning him and the other apostles to extend and rule it (cf. Matt. 28:18, etc.) ... constituted and organized as a society in the present world, subsists in the Catholic Church [*subsistit in Ecclesia catholica*], which is governed by the successor of Peter and by the bishops in communion with him" (LG 8). It would seem that an important key for interpreting this text is offered in UR 4, which says that "the unity of the one and only Church, which Christ bestowed on his Church from the beginning ... we believe subsists in the Catholic Church [*in Ecclesia catholica subsistere credimus*]." The subsistence of the structure of unity and leadership established in Peter and the apostles is intrinsic to the subsistence of the church itself.

the college "preserves intact his function [*munus*] as Vicar of Christ and pastor of the universal Church." The council thus teaches that there are two not entirely distinct subjects of supreme power in the church, namely "the Roman Pontiff by himself and the Roman Pontiff along with the bishops" (LG, *Nota* 3). Vatican II also taught that there are two not entirely distinct subjects of infallibility, namely the pope himself and the college of bishops united in communion with one another and with the successor of Peter, either "dispersed throughout the world" or, more specifically, "assembled in an ecumenical council" (LG 25).

There has long been discussion as to whether, both in the case of supreme power and in the case of infallibility, these two subjects might in fact be understood as just one. At the time of Vatican I, many thought that there was indeed only one subject, namely the pope, and that bishops participated in his power and councils participated in his infallibility. Just before Vatican II, however, Karl Rahner offered a different solution. He proposed that there is only one subject of supreme power and of infallibility in the church, and that that one subject is "the college of bishops united under the pope as its head." It is the college, including the pope as a constitutive element, which acts in an ecumenical council, and the pope, even when acting alone, "still acts *as* head of the episcopal college."[34]

34. Karl Rahner, "On the Divine Right of the Episcopate," in Karl Rahner and Joseph Ratzinger, *The Episcopate and the Primacy* (New York: Herder and Herder, 1962), 64–135, here at 92–101.

This view comes very close to seeing the pope as a corporate personality, as was suggested above,[35] summing up in his own person the college of bishops, and it seems to accord well with the scriptural data regarding the Twelve and Peter. There is no pope without the episcopal college of which he is a member, and there is no college without its head, the pope. Congar later summarized in similar terms what Vatican II taught: "there was no episcopate without the Pope and no Pope without the episcopate."[36] Rahner proposed that: "The pope is pope (supreme and immediate pastor of the whole Church) precisely *insofar* as he is head of the college of bishops"; the latter role is not simply added on to the former, it *grounds* the former.[37]

Rahner also maintained that his view did "ample justice" to the teaching of Vatican I that the infallible definitions of the pope are irreformable "of themselves and not from the consent of the Church [*ex sese non autem ex consensu ecclesiae*]."[38] That phrase, "*ex sese non autem ex consensu ecclesiae*," is still often misunderstood as implying that the pope is cut off from the church and that his teaching is independent of the faith of the church. In fact, however, it was introduced for a specific purpose, namely to deny the claims of Gallicanism (in-

35. Cf. above, pp. 18–19, 21, 26.

36. Yves Congar, "A Last Look at the Council," in Alberic Stacpoole, ed., *Vatican II by those who were there* (London: Geoffrey Chapman, 1986), 337–58, here at 343. Cf. RD 43: "Primacy and conciliarity are mutually interdependent."

37. Rahner, "On the Divine Right of the Episcopate," 99.

38. Rahner, "On the Divine Right of the Episcopate," 97; cf. Vatican I, *Pastor Aeternus*, ch.4, DH 3074.

fluenced by conciliarism) that papal decisions required the express consent of the bishops in order to be binding for the whole church.[39] Such a view rests on a mistaken understanding of the relationship between the pope and the bishops, viewing these as two separate entities, not integrated as one in the way Rahner indicates. If they are separated, then the question naturally arises as to which has priority, the pope or the bishops? The *per Petrum* idea says that the bishops receive their power of jurisdiction from the pope, and thus makes them secondary to the pope. Gallicanism and conciliarism take the opposite view, maintaining that the jurisdiction of the bishops comes directly from God, and that they "govern their dioceses independently."[40] Thus, the pope's jurisdiction is operative only secondarily and requires the bishops' consent for its exercise. In their different ways, both of these views are mistaken, because, in reality, as Rahner maintains, pope and bishops are simultaneous; the existence of each implies the other, and papal and episcopal authority condition one another, both being of divine institution. It follows, as already seen, that there is therefore a "fundamental *mutual interiority* between universal Church and particular Church" (CN 13).[41]

39. Cf. Henn, "Historical-Theological Synthesis," 222–73, at 253, 254, 261. Also, Hermann J. Pottmeyer, *Towards a Papacy in Communion: Perspectives from Vatican Councils I & II* (New York: Herder and Herder, 1998), 68, 102. Vatican I firmly rejected conciliarism when it said that it was erroneous to believe that "it is permitted to appeal to an ecumenical Council from the decisions of the Roman Pontiff, as to an authority superior to the Roman Pontiff" (DH 3063; ND, 318–19).

40. Henn, "Historical-Theological Synthesis," 254.

41. Cf. above, p. 23.

Acknowledging that the "*ex sese*" of Vatican I is a "harsh and very ambiguous formula," Ratzinger nonetheless believes that it is an attempt to express something of great importance, namely, the specific calling and charism that the pope and the bishops have in order to give authentic voice to the faith of the church, even or perhaps especially in situations of "confusion" in the church, when "consensus is lacking." He stresses that "the teaching ministry always acts against the background of the faith and prayer of the whole Church," but adds, however, that "its office is not reduced merely to ratifying the assent already expressed by the latter, indeed, in the interpretation and explanation of the written or transmitted word of God, the Magisterium can anticipate or demand their assent."[42] Vatican II similarly refers not only to the faith of the church but also to the responsibility of the magisterium when it indicates two particular ways in which "the Tradition which comes from the apostles makes progress in the Church, with the help of the Holy Spirit," namely, "through the contemplation and study of believers" and also "from the preaching of those who have received, along with the right of succession in the episcopate, the sure charism of truth" (DV 8).[43] What is particularly significant in Ratzinger's explanation above of the *ex sese*, which was used by Vatican I solely with reference

42. Joseph Ratzinger, *Principles of Catholic Theology* (San Francisco: Ignatius, 1987), 234. The final quotation is taken from the Declaration in Defense of the Catholic Doctrine on the Church against Some Present-Day Errors, *Mysterium Ecclesiae,* issued by the CDF in 1973.

43. Though not cited here by the council, it was Irenaeus who spoke of the *charisma veritatis certum* of the bishops in apostolic succession; *Adv. Haer.* 4, 26, 2.

to *papal* teaching, is that he implicitly speaks of the pope and the bishops *together*, by referring simply to "the teaching ministry" and "the Magisterium" of the church.[44] He himself thereby shows that pope and bishops are never to be considered apart.

In fact, Vatican I clearly excluded any idea that papal teaching was independent of the faith of the church by stating that the infallibility that the pope exercises under certain carefully specified conditions is the infallibility with which Christ "willed his Church to be endowed" (DH 3074). It was clarified in the conciliar debate that this power is not personally possessed by the pope, but simply given as an assistance when he speaks *ex cathedra*, that is, in and for the church.[45] What is fundamental is the infallibility of the church; the pope has this prerogative "as he *represents* the Church": "there is only one infallibility and Christ promised infallibility to the entire magisterium of the church, to the apostles united to Peter."[46] It is highly significant in this regard that the two infallible pronouncements of recent times, regarding

44. Ratzinger, *Principles of Catholic Theology*, 234.

45. It is because Pope Honorius, who was anathematized by Constantinople III for endorsing monothelite views, did so only in a letter to Patriarch Sergius and not in a solemn *ex cathedra* pronouncement that his action does not serve as a contradiction of papal infallibility.

46. Maurice C. Duchaine, "Vatican I on Primacy and Infallibility," in Empie and Murphy, eds., *Papal Primacy and the Universal Church*, 139–50, 148–49, with reference to Bishop Gasser's explanation of infallibility during the course of Vatican I. Vatican II also referred to Gasser's explanation when it stated that, when making an infallible definition, the pope does not speak "as a private person, but rather does he expound and defend the teaching of the Catholic faith as the supreme teacher of the universal Church, in whom the Church's charism of infallibility is present in a singular way" (LG 25, and note 43).

the Immaculate Conception of the Blessed Virgin Mary (1854) and Mary's Assumption (1950), were both preceded by an extensive inquiry among the bishops and the faithful to determine the faith of the church.[47]

It is a great misfortune that Vatican I was adjourned for political reasons when only part of its planned teaching on the church had been completed. The council's document, *Pastor Aeternus*, specifically called the *first* dogmatic constitution on the church, and deliberately restricted to teaching about the pope, was always intended to be complemented by a *second* dogmatic constitution on the church, *Tametsi Deus*, which would deal more fully with the bishops and with the Church at large. The second constitution was drafted by Joseph Kleutgen but never distributed and debated. The continuity between Vatican I and II in this vital area of doctrine is clear from the many citations of the teaching of *Pastor Aeternus* in ch.3 of *Lumen Gentium*, "On the Hierarchical Constitution of the Church and especially on the Episcopate," and from the fact that the footnotes to ch.3 contain references not only to the reports that Bishop Gasser and Bishop Zinelli gave at Vatican I explaining the exact meaning and context of *Pastor Aeternus* (cf. LG, notes 43, 44, 45, 46 and 27, 28, 60, respectively), but also to the draft second constitution of Vatican I and to Kleutgen's *Relatio* explaining that text (cf. LG, notes 28, 40).

The lack of a completed second constitution deprived Catholic teaching of equilibrium with regard to primacy and episcopacy after Vatican I; there was a strong em-

47. Cf. J. M. R. Tillard, "Sensus Fidelium," *One in Christ* 11 (1975), 2–29.

phasis on the pope and primacy without a complementary emphasis on the bishops and collegiality or conciliarity. The declaration of the German hierarchy (1875) in response to allegations by Bismarck that the teaching of Vatican I had reduced bishops to mere executives of the pope insisted, however, that both the papacy and the episcopate were of divine institution and that the pope had neither the right nor the power to change the rights and duties of the episcopate. Thus, as the declaration said, it was a complete misunderstanding to imagine that episcopal jurisdiction had been absorbed into papal jurisdiction (DH 3115). Pope Pius IX expressly endorsed the declaration as expressing the authentic meaning of Vatican I (DH 3117). It may be said, nevertheless, that the legalistic formulation of Vatican I, whereby each bishop had ordinary and immediate episcopal jurisdiction over his own flock (DH 3061), and the pope had ordinary and immediate episcopal jurisdiction over the church as a whole (DH 3060), was liable to the very misunderstanding that the German bishops condemned. When Vatican II returned to this issue, it used a *sacramental* vocabulary enriched by the biblical, patristic, and liturgical renewals of the twentieth century in order to present the same doctrine much more satisfactorily. The word "jurisdiction" actually has relatively little prominence in the teaching of Vatican II,[48] and the 1985 Extraordinary Assembly of the Synod of Bishops, called to reflect on the council's legacy, stated firmly that "the theology of collegiality is much

48. Cf. Henn, "Historical-Theological Synthesis," 267.

more extensive than its mere juridical aspect." The Synod fathers wanted indeed to draw attention to "the sacramental foundation of collegiality" that was provided by the "ecclesiology of communion."[49]

With regard to the teaching of Vatican I, even without the balancing content of a second constitution on the church, it is important to note various points, as follows. First, the council taught that the primacy exists "so that the episcopate itself might be one and undivided, and that the whole multitude of believers might be preserved in unity of faith and communion [*in fidei et communione unitate*] by means of a closely united priesthood" (DH 3051; cf. LG 18).[50] Thus the life of the church was already recognized as one of *communion*, and the importance of the episcopate itself being one and undivided was stressed in that context. Christ, said the Council, "placed St. Peter at the head of the other apostles, and established in him a perpetual and visible foundation of this twofold unity" (DH 3051; cf. LG 23). As the successor of Peter, therefore, the pope's task is to serve the church's unity in faith and communion. In addition, the council quoted the papal legate at the Council of Ephesus (431) and also Pope Leo I's teaching that Peter himself still lives and guides the church in his successors (DH 3056, 3057), and it said that when the pope speaks infallibly he does so thanks to the divine assistance

49. Extraordinary Assembly of the Synod of Bishops (1985), *Final Relatio*, II, C, 4.

50. The translations of Vatican I texts in this and the following two paragraphs are taken from ND, 314–22.

"promised to him in the person of Blessed Peter [*in beato Petro*]" (DH 3074). Thus the patristic idea of the pope as vicar of Peter was still strongly present. The council also quoted St. Irenaeus, that every church should be in agreement with the Roman Church "on account of its pre-eminence [*propter potentiorem principalitatem*]," and St Ambrose, that from the see of Rome "the bonds of sacred communion [*venerandae communionis iura*]" are imparted to all (DH 3057),[51] thereby reinforcing an awareness that Rome is the center of the church's twofold unity in faith and in communion.

Vatican I reaffirmed the definition given by the Council of Florence of the pope's "primacy over the whole world" and headship of the whole church (DH 3059), but it also quoted St. Gregory the Great ("My honor is the honor of the whole Church. My honor is the firm strength of my brothers")[52] to stress that papal power does not deny but supports episcopal jurisdiction (DH 3061; cf. LG 27). With regard to infallibility, it referred to the Fourth Council of Constantinople (869–70), and to the *Libellus satisfactionis* that was signed there,[53] largely based on the profession of faith that Pope Hormisdas originally sent to Constantinople in 515 to be signed by those returning to communion after the Acacian Schism. The profession recognized the unsullied faith of the apostolic see

51. Cf. Irenaeus, *Adv. Haer.* 3, 3, 2; Ambrose, *Ep.* 11, 4. The phrase of Irenaeus, difficult to translate, is perhaps a reference to the unique distinction of Rome as the place of martyrdom of the two *princes* of the apostles, Peter and Paul.

52. Cf. above, pp. 21–22.

53. Cf. above, p. 32.

in accordance with the Lord's promise to Peter in Matt. 16:18 and expressed the desire be in communion with that see (DH 3066 and 363–65; cf. above, §25). Vatican I also quoted the Second Council of Lyons, and the Council of Florence again, in saying that the Roman see and its bishop received the primacy and the power of teaching and defending the truth of faith "in the person of blessed Peter [*in beato Petro*]" (DH 3067, 3068). Summing up both millennia, but specifically looking back to the first, it said that the idea that the power of teaching was contained in the pope's primacy over the whole church was something that "the perpetual practice of the Church confirms, and the ecumenical Councils, especially those in which the Western and Eastern Churches were united in faith and love" (DH 3065).

By these manifold references and citations, drawn from both the first and the second millennium, Vatican I showed its firm desire to teach what had always been believed and taught, especially in the time of the undivided church, regarding the pope and the bishops, and not to make any innovations. Indeed, it explicitly said in the introduction to *Pastor Aeternus* that it wished to propose what was to be believed and held "according to the ancient and constant belief of the universal Church" (DH 3052). The particular shape of the council's teaching, with its strong, monarchical accent on the papacy, was prompted by the extreme situation of the time, when, as Cardinal Walter Kasper says, many regarded the church as "besieged from all sides and in an almost apocalyptic situation." It was judged necessary to define the pope's primacy "in such a way that he could act even if he were to be prevented from communicating with the Church." The council's teaching was thus "especially conceived for extreme and exceptional situations."[54] Nevertheless, its teaching was meant to accord with what the universal church had always believed, and it is therefore legitimate to view and to interpret Vatican I "in the context of the older Councils." In fact, as a general principle, each council, guided by one and the same Holy Spirit, "is to be interpreted in the light of the whole tradition and of all the Councils." "What was true in the first millennium cannot be untrue in the second."[55]

Given, therefore, the strong continuity with the teaching of earlier councils that Vatican I intended in its own teaching, as just seen; and also given the continuity, noted above, between Vatican I and Vatican II, which itself pointed back to earlier times and directed that Catholic-Orthodox reconciliation should be sought with attentiveness to "the character of the relations which obtained between [the Eastern Churches] and the Roman See before the separation" (UR 14), it is appropriate now to ask what *was* the situation, before the separation of 1054, with regard to primacy and conciliarity? Vatican I, implicitly, and Vatican II, explicitly, both indicate that the understanding and practices of the first millennium can serve as pointers for the future.

54. Walter Kasper, "Introduction to the Theme and Catholic Hermeneutics of the Dogmas of the First Vatican Council," in Cardinal Walter Kasper, ed., *The Petrine Ministry: Catholics and Orthodox in Dialogue* (New York/Mahwah, N.J.: Newman Press, 2006), 7–23, here at 19.

55. Kasper, "Introduction to the Theme," 17.

3

THE FIRST MILLENNIUM
AND THE FUTURE

In his examination of papal authority in the first four centuries, Pierre Battifol distinguished "three zones" for separate consideration: the suburbicarian area immediately subject to Rome, the West in general beyond that area, and the East. In each of the three zones, the church of Rome exercised both *sollicitudo* (solicitude) and *potestas* (power), but in profoundly different ways. With regard to the two Western zones, there were differing measures of papal jurisdiction. With regard to the East, however, relations were determined by three factors: the "preeminence [*précellence*] of the faith of the church of Rome," the "canonical autonomy of the East," and "the necessity of the East being in communion with the church of Rome."[1]

All through the first millennium, new archbishops of Constantinople, Alexandria, and Antioch would announce their election to the bishop of Rome "to obtain his communion," but the East never wanted the "subjection" that Rome required of the West. Rome accepted this fact and, in its relations with the East, was con-

1. Cf. Pierre Battifol, *Cathedra Petri* (Paris: Cerf, 1938), 41, 61, 75.

cerned simply for the preservation of orthodoxy and communion. The bishop of Rome had outstanding authority in the East, but it was never understood as an authority "by divine right," and in particular the East never shared the West's basic understanding of the link between the bishop of Rome and Peter, whereby the bishop of Rome was not just Peter's successor but "Peter perpetuated, invested with his responsibility and his power,"[2] that is "vicar of Peter," as indicated above.[3]

Two points may be noted here: first, while there is continuity between Leo I's patristic idea that the pope is vicar of Peter and heir to his unique *consortium* with Christ on the one hand, and the understanding of Boniface VIII (1294–1303), typical of the second millennium, that the pope is successor of Peter and vicar of Christ on the other hand.[4] There is also a distinction between these views. Ullmann emphasizes the difference between "apostolic succession" in the latter case and what he calls "juristic succession" in the former: in juristic succession, "no pope succeeds another pope, but succeeds St Peter immediately."[5] It may perhaps be said that juristic succession is more iconic, even potentially eschatological, whereas apostolic succession is more pronouncedly historical. Second, it is with regard to Battifol's third zone,

2. Battifol, *Cathedra Petri*, 75–76. Battifol regrets that such a decisive issue as the role and authority of the bishop of Rome was not resolved by an ecumenical council in the period of the undivided church.

3. Cf. above, p. 23.

4. Cf. Boniface VIII, Bull *Unam Sanctam* (1302): "The one and unique Church is one body with one head, not two heads like a monster, namely Christ and the vicar of Christ, Peter and Peter's successor" (DH 872).

5. Ullmann, "Leo I and the Theme of Papal Primacy," 28, 50.

namely the East, that the specific characteristics of the pope's role as universal *primate* can be discerned. The juridical role he plays in the West is not to be confused with the primatial role he exercises for the church both West and East. In that light, it appears that the essence of *primacy* is concern for the church's unity in faith (orthodoxy) and communion.[6]

In the first millennium, both in the West and in the East, the pope was recognized as having a primacy of honor (he was "first in honor"),[7] and Rome always appeared first in the canonical order or *taxis* of the major sees: Rome, Constantinople, Alexandria, Antioch, Jerusalem (cf. RD 35, 40, 41). As Brian Daley has shown, the phrase, "primacy of honor," first used by the second ecumenical council (Constantinople, 381) to refer to the privileges of the bishop of Constantinople after the bishop of Rome, implies not just an honorific position, but real "prerogatives of office," such that the phrase is best understood as meaning "the honour of primacy" or "the status of seniority."[8] Vlassios Phidas understands the phrase as associated with "an exceptional authority *(singularis auctoritas)*, which consists in guaranteeing the

6. Cf. Vatican I, DH 3051; above, pp. 49–50.

7. Cf. above, pp. 27, 39–40.

8. Brian E. Daley, "Position and Patronage in the Early Church: The Original Meaning of 'Primacy of Honour,'" in *Journal of Theological Studies* 44 (1993), 529–53, here at 534, 542. Pope Benedict XVI highlights this point when he says that the phrase "first among equals" needs to be treated with some caution: "it acknowledges that the Bishop of Rome is the *protos*, the first, as is laid down already by the Council of Nicaea. But the question is precisely whether the Pope has specific tasks or not"; *The Light of the World: A Conversation with Peter Seewald* (San Francisco: Ignatius Press, 2010), 88–89.

unity of the Church in the true faith and in the canonical discipline." Accordingly, "in the order of precedence of the patriarchal sees, the *prima sedes* has a particular role in the manner in which the patriarchal pentarchy functions." "The bishop of the 'first see' takes the presidency in an ecumenical council, and his authority is exercised in the life of the Church."[9] As was seen above, Nicetas indeed recognized the bishop of Rome as having first place in an ecumenical council and as exercising additional responsibilities in the life of the church, such as resolving appeals and settling disputes.[10]

In the teaching of Vatican II, three particular primatial prerogatives of the bishop of Rome are identified which closely align with the reality of the first millennium as described by Battifol and Phidas and with the convictions of Nicetas still in the twelfth century, namely: moderating disputes, presiding at ecumenical councils, and serving the (Eucharistic) communion of the local churches in one church. These will now be considered in turn, and the teaching of Vatican II in each case will be illustrated from the first millennium.

Moderating Disputes

In its decree on ecumenism, Vatican II said: "For many centuries the Churches of the East and of the West went their own ways, though a brotherly communion of faith and sacramental life bound them together. If dis-

9. Phidas, "Papal Primacy and Patriarchal Pentarchy in the Orthodox Tradition," 74.
10. Cf. above, p. 39.

agreements in faith and discipline arose among them, the Roman See acted by common consent as moderator" (UR 14).[11] Klaus Schatz similarly comments that most of the "papal initiatives outside of the ecclesiastical province of Rome" in the first millennium consisted of responses to "requests and pleas."[12]

The case of St Athanasius (c.296–373) exemplifies this service by the Roman see.[13] After the Council of Nicaea, Arianism continued to trouble the Church gravely in the East, and orthodox bishops were ousted from the leading sees of Alexandria, Antioch, and Constantinople by anti-Nicene forces. Eusebius, bishop of Nicomedia and subsequently bishop of Constantinople (339), was prominent in such activities. Athanasius, who became bishop of Alexandria in 328, was condemned by a council at Tyre in 335. He returned from exile in 337, but Eusebius wrote to Pope Julius (337–52) urging him to withdraw communion from Athanasius on the grounds of the latter's condemnation by the council at Tyre. Athanasius convoked a council at Alexandria in 338 which produced an encyclical letter defending him, and this letter, sent to

11. Cf. the statement later in UR 14: "the heritage handed down by the apostles was received differently and in different forms, so that from the very beginnings of the Church its development varied from region to region and also because of differing mentalities and ways of life."

12. Klaus Schatz, *Il primato del papa* (Brescia: Queriniana, 1996), 125; quoted by Henn, "Historical-Theological synthesis," 230.

13. The main sources for details of the controversy are Athanasius's own *Historia Arianorum* and *Apologia contra Arianos*, and the histories written by Theodoret, Socrates, and Sozomen. The following summary draws particularly on Manlio Simonetti, *La crisi ariana nel IV secolo* (Roma: Institutum Patristicum «Augustinianum», 1975), and Dom John Chapman, *Studies on the Early Papacy* (London: Sheed & Ward, 1928).

the whole church, was taken to Rome by envoys who encountered there the envoys of Eusebius. It is not known exactly what was said by the Eusebians, but Pope Julius interpreted it as a request to refer the whole matter to a council, and he then wrote both to Athanasius and to his opponents proposing the holding of a council.[14] The Eusebians, gathered in council at Antioch, conducted a highly irregular election of a new bishop, Gregory, for Alexandria, and Athanasius was again deposed. He duly arrived in Rome toward the end of 339, but his opponents never came. Instead, they eventually sent a letter saying that there was no need for a council since all the contentious issues had been properly resolved.[15]

The synod finally took place in Rome in the spring of 341. The bishops confirmed their communion with Athanasius, overturning the synod of Tyre, and Julius sent a severe letter in the name of the council to Athanasius's opponents saying that if suspicion had fallen upon the bishop of Alexandria a letter should have been written to the church of Rome. The "ecclesiastical canon" and the "traditions of the Fathers" had been violated by the actions of the Eusebians: "I beseech you to hear willingly what I say, for I write for the common welfare, and what we have received from Blessed Peter the Apostle, that I declare to you."[16] The historians, Socrates and Sozomen, say that Julius also wrote letters restoring other East-

14. Cf. Simonetti, *La crisi ariana nel IV secolo*, 141.

15. Cf. ibid., 145.

16. Letter reproduced in Athanasius, *Apologia contra Arianos* 20–35, here at 35 (PG 25b, 307A–B); translation from Chapman, *Studies on the Early Papacy*, 58.

ern bishops to their sees because of the prerogatives of Rome and "on the ground that the care of all belonged to him."[17] None of these decisions were implemented, however, because the East was under the control of the Arian Emperor Constantius. Athanasius himself remained in Rome. Pope Julius and others suggested to the Western emperor, Constans, that he write to his brother Constantius and arrange a great synod of West and East to resolve all disputed matters, especially the case of Athanasius. The council duly met at Sardica, just inside the Western Empire, in 343, with Athanasius in attendance.

The main issue at Sardica was one of due order and process in the church with regard to charges against bishops, there being as yet no fixed procedure in such cases. Could the decision of the synod of Tyre or of any synod be overturned by another synod, and what role might the bishop of Rome have? The recent council at Antioch in 341, attended only by Eastern bishops and the Emperor Constantius, had agreed a limited right of appeal: a condemned bishop could appeal to bishops of the neighboring province if the judgment of bishops in his own province was not unanimous. That, however, would not have helped Athanasius, and Sardica duly crafted a more significant right of appeal. The Eastern bishops attending Sardica objected to the presence of Athanasius and said that no synod could overturn another, and no bishop could appeal from a first condemnation. This view was rejected by the others, and the Easterners withdrew, subsequently writing their own condemnation of Julius.

17. Chapman, *Studies on the Early Papacy*, 59.

The synod at Sardica continued, however, presided over by Bishop Hosius of Cordova, and with two papal legates present. Notably saying that it wished to "honour the memory of the most holy Apostle Peter," it agreed that various canons would govern appeals by bishops. If a bishop considered he had been unjustly judged, then the bishops trying the case, or neighboring bishops, could write to the bishop of Rome. The bishop of Rome could then decide whether the decision should stand or if there should be a retrial, in which case he would appoint judges (canon 3). If a bishop was accused and deposed by his fellow bishops and then appealed to Rome, the bishop of Rome could write to the bishops of the neighboring province and ask them to give judgment; if he wished he could send a presbyter, with the authority of the bishop of Rome, to sit with the bishops and give judgment with them (canon 5).[18]

The lengthy controversy shows that even Eusebius himself recognized, by writing his initial letter to Pope Julius, that the bishop of Rome did have a role of some sort to play in the affairs of the church in the East, and especially in Eastern disputes. What that role was, however, and specifically whether the bishop of Rome could hold a council to hear an appeal, was still unclear in the East. History shows, in fact, that an orthodox bishop was likely to be replaced during his absence to attend such a council, and to be forbidden by the Arian emperor to return. Sardica agreed something much more

18. Cf. J. Stevenson, *Creeds, Councils and Controversies: Documents Illustrating the History of the Church, AD 337–461* (London: SPCK, 1987), 15–16.

practical, namely that the pope could order a new trial in the territory of the accused bishop. Dom John Chapman considers that such "extraordinary powers" indicate that the pope was far more than just an "honorary primate," and seem to indicate that, with significant reference to St Peter, the pope was recognized at Sardica as having "a duty of general guardianship over the whole Church."[19]

Bernard Dupuy sees already in the actions of Julius and the council of Antioch, respectively, the beginnings of "two ecclesiologies, Western and Eastern," and considers that Sardica successfully mediated between them. "The council of Sardica did not admit the regionalist and provincialist jurisprudence of the council of Antioch in 341, but neither did it endorse the primatial sense that Julius seems to have had in affirming the principle of Rome's right to consider *all major episcopal causes* before judgment." Sardica did not give the pope himself the right with his synod to judge in all situations of conflict; instead, it recognized "a right of appeal to Rome" under set conditions, whereby the bishop of Rome could entrust judgment to neighboring bishops, with some delegates of his own participating if he wished.[20] East and West were subsequently treated in different ways, nevertheless. Pope Innocent I (401–17) required that major cases in the West be referred to Rome after local episcopal judgment, but saw himself simply as an "arbitrator" in Eastern cases, without the right of "intervention or final judgment."[21]

19. Chapman, *Studies on the Early Papacy*, 67–68.

20. Bernard Dupuy, "Les appels de l'Orient à Rome du concile de Nicée au concile de Chalcédoine," *Istina* 32 (1987), 361–77, here at 368–69.

21. Ibid., 370–71.

Hervé Legrand similarly notes the subtlety of Sardica's decision. The council acknowledged Rome as having a primacy but not a sovereignty—it could not judge cases itself; instead, it had the power to review a case and send it for appeal. Thus, Rome had what he calls a "primacy in communion."[22] Moreover, he notes that most *but not all* of the Eastern bishops left the council; only Athanasius's Antiochian adversaries left, about eighty in number. So the council should not be too hastily categorized as simply a *Western* council; in principle, it was a council of the whole Empire, and it was received not only in the West but also in the East.[23] Its canons [24] were officially received in the East at the council *in Trullo* (692), and they subsequently played a role in the Photian controversy. Even though Patriarch Ignatius (c.797–877) of Constantinople, deposed by the emperor in 858 in favor of Photius (c.810–c.95), had not appealed to Rome, the legates of Pope Nicholas I (858–67) to the synod of Constantinople (861) invoked Sardica to justify their re-examination of the case of Ignatius, and Photius's supporters accepted their right to do so.[25] This shows that Sardica was by then accepted in Constantinople.[26] The synod deposed Ignati-

22. Hervé Legrand, "Pour une approche procédurale de la primauté romaine," *Istina* 53 (2008), 23–46, here at 28–29, 35.

23. Ibid., 28, 32.

24. Henn notes several occasions when subsequent popes mistakenly attributed to the council of Nicaea the canons of Sardica regarding appeals by bishops; William Henn, *The Honor of My Brothers: A Short History of the Relations between the Pope and the Bishops* (New York: Crossroad Publishing Company, 2000), 57.

25. Legrand, "Pour une approche," 34.

26. Cf. Francis Dvornik, *Byzantium and the Roman Primacy* (New York: Fordham University Press, 1966), 109.

us, but Nicholas's legates had exceeded their powers, and a synod at Rome (863) annulled the verdict of the synod of 861 and supported Ignatius. After a delegation from Ignatius arrived in Rome, Pope Nicholas deposed Photius and declared the deposition of Ignatius null and void. However, Nicholas himself had now exceeded his powers as far as Sardica was concerned, and his assertion of a juridical power in the East,[27] provoked Eastern protest. Another council at Constantinople in 867 declared the pope anathema. This protracted dispute led to a considerable worsening in relations between East and West, in spite of the subsequent reconciliations achieved at the council of 869–70 in favor of Ignatius, and at the council of 879–80 in favor of Photius.[28]

Though it is little regarded now, Legrand urges that Sardica, rightly considered, has "exceptional ecclesiological and ecumenical interest," because it is "the only council where the Churches of the East (including Photius) and of the West recognized the principle of a primacy in the midst of the Church and gave it a definite form." Sardica determined that within the fundamental conciliarity of the church there was a right of appeal to the bishop of Rome, located at the center of the communion of the church and exercising "an authority in communion."[29]

27. Cf. above, p. 39, note 30; also p. 32, note 10, for Pope Hadrian II soon afterwards.

28. The former is regarded in the West as the eighth ecumenical council, namely the fourth Council of Constantinople, but its status is somewhat dubious. The latter is regarded by a considerable body of opinion, both Catholic and Orthodox, as being truly the eighth ecumenical council; cf. Congar, *Diversity and Communion*, 93.

29. Legrand, "Pour une approche," 34–35.

Sardica also indicated that the pope was the final arbiter in ecclesial disputes, not the emperor, and thus equipped the church for a time when there would no longer be an emperor.[30] More fundamentally, it equipped the church for an existence independent of the state, whose emperors and rulers are by no means always reliable as champions of orthodoxy, as the multiple Arian and iconoclast emperors of the first millennium demonstrate. Pope Benedict comments:

During the first three centuries Rome was the headquarters and capital of the Christian persecutions. Withstanding these persecutions and giving witness to Christ was the special task of the Roman episcopal see. We can regard it as providential that at the moment when Christianity entered a period of peace with the State, the imperial throne was transferred to Constantinople on the Bosphorus. Thus the Bishop of Rome could more easily set forth the independence of the Church, the fact that she is distinct from the State.[31]

A striking feature of the crises relating to Athanasius and Photius is that both show the bishop of Rome acting in concert with a Roman synod or council. This was a constant feature of Roman practice. Pope Damasus held a synod at Rome in 371 to condemn the Arian creed of the Council of Rimini in 359.[32] After the Coun-

30. Cf. ibid., 35–36.
31. Pope Benedict XVI, *Light of the World*, 9. Pottmeyer highlights the recurrent importance of this theme in the West: "As in the eleventh century, so also in the nineteenth, the struggle of the popes for the independence of the church was an important reason for the strengthening of the papal primacy of jurisdiction" (*Towards a Papacy in Communion*, 28–29).
32. Cf. Henn, *The Honor of My Brothers*, 57.

cil of Constantinople (381) placed Constantinople next in rank after Rome "because that city is a new Rome" (canon 3), thus seemingly basing primacy on civil importance, Damasus held another council in Rome in 382 which affirmed that primacy was based on Christ's commissioning of Peter, and that Rome, Alexandria, and Antioch had their prominence in the church because they were all Petrine sees.[33] After Cyril of Alexandria (patriarch, 412–44) sought Pope Celestine's support against Nestorius, who became patriarch of Constantinople in 428, the pope held a synod in 430 which approved the title of "Mother of God" (*Theotokos*) for Mary, and Pope Celestine (422–32) then authorized Cyril to act in his place and with the authority of Rome to enforce Nestorius's adherence to orthodox doctrine. While Celestine seems to have regarded his own synod as having sufficient authority in this matter, Nestorius appealed to the emperor for the holding of an ecumenical council, duly held at Ephesus in 431, which nevertheless recognized the importance of Celestine's letter in its own judgment.[34] Again in 680, after a series of Western synods ordered by the pope to consider the monothelite controversy, Pope Agatho held a synod in Rome which composed a profession of faith condemning monothelitism, and papal legates took this profession to the Third Council of Constantinople where it was adopted.[35]

Even though the significance of the bishop of Rome's actions in these various important cases affecting the

33. Cf. ibid., 59–60. 34. Cf. ibid., 67–68.
35. Cf. above, p. 24.

faith and communion of the church was sometimes assessed differently in East and West, respectively, what is evident is that the pope consistently acted synodically.[36] Indeed in correspondence during the Photian dispute, bishops of Rome repeatedly emphasized that they had taken their decisions in accordance with the rules or canons, and had acted synodically (*"synodice regulariterque"* or *"canonice ac synodice"*).[37] The first millennium thus shows the bishops of Rome playing an important role in moderating disputes in the church both West and East in various ways, with significant canonical determinations being given at Sardica. It can be said, however, that this prerogative was normally exercised synodically.

Presiding at Ecumenical Councils

Vatican II affirmed that:

The supreme authority [*suprema potestas*] over the whole Church, which [the college of bishops] possesses, is exercised in a solemn way in an ecumenical council. There never is an ecumenical council which is not confirmed or at least recognized as such by Peter's successor. And it is the prerogative of the Roman Pontiff to convoke such councils, to preside over them and to confirm them (LG 22).

36. Mansi vol. 36A, "Conspectus Collectionis Conciliorum Mansi et Continuatorum," 3–151, records 186 synods and councils in Rome in the period c.136–1234. Adrian Fortescue explains that there were two kinds of *concilium apostolicae sedis*: the first was made up of the "suburban bishops, the Roman parish priests, and regionary deacons" who formed "a permanent institution" around the pope, and second, there were also "specially summoned Roman provincial synods"; "Holy Synod," *The Catholic Encyclopedia*, vol.7 (New York: The Gilmary Society, 1913), 428–32, here at 428.

37. Nicholas I, Letter, 13 Nov. 866, *Monumenta Germaniae Historica* (MGH), *Epistolarum tomus* VI (1978), 523; Hadrian II, Letter, 10 June 869,

Though the convoking of ecumenical councils by the bishop of Rome is something first seen in the twelfth century the first millennium consistently shows that the involvement of the bishop of Rome in some capacity was a necessary condition for the ecumenicity of a council: "no ecumenical council has *ever* been considered as such without the collaboration of or reception by Rome."[38]

The major contributions of Pope Celestine to the Council of Ephesus, Pope Leo to the Council of Chalcedon, and Pope Agatho to the Third Council of Constantinople have already been mentioned, and the contribution of Pope Hadrian I to the Second Council of Nicaea (787) is highly significant also. The latter council endorsed the pope's teaching on the veneration of icons expressed in his letter to the Empress Irene. The pope accepted the Empress's invitation to send two legates to the council only on condition that the iconoclastic synod of Hiereia (754) be condemned. By way of refuting the ecumenical character of Hiereia, Nicaea II duly gave the clearest statement yet formulated of the criteria necessary for a council to be recognized as ecumenical. Five criteria for an ecumenical council were indicated: the council has to be accepted by the heads of the churches, and they have to be in agreement (*symphonia*) with it; "the pope of the Romans" has to be a "co-operator" or "fellow worker" (*synergos*) with the council, at least by

MGH, *Ep.* VI, 751. Cf. de Vries, *Orient et Occident*, 248, 267, 268, 269, 270; "the authority of the bishop of Rome over the universal Church was understood at that time, by the East as well as the West, as an authority which was exercised, at least normally, in a synodal manner" (270).

38. Legrand, "Pour une approche", 39.

letter or via representatives, "as the law of councils requires"; the patriarchs of the East (Alexandria, Antioch, and Jerusalem, "the holy city," were named; Constantinople was taken as read) have to be "in agreement" (*symphronountes*); the teaching of the council must accord with that of previous "holy and venerable" ecumenical councils; and the council must have its own proper number in the sequence of councils recognized and accepted by the church.[39] The involvement of the pope is clearly treated as a condition for ecumenicity here, though scholarly discussion continues regarding the nuances of the terminology and the circumstances of the time.

Patriarch Nicephorus (758–828) of Constantinople subsequently emphasized the importance of Rome's participation at Nicaea II, which gave that council an authority not possessed by Hiereia:

This Synod possesses the highest authority.... In fact it was held in the most legitimate and regular fashion conceivable, because according to the divine rules established from the beginning it was directed and presided over by that glorious portion of the Western Church, I mean by the Church of Ancient Rome. Without them [the Romans], no dogma discussed in the Church, even sanctioned in a preliminary fashion by the canons and ecclesiastical usages, can be considered to be approved, or abrogated; for they are the ones, in fact, who possess the principate of the priesthood and who owe this distinction to the two leaders of the Apostles.[40]

---

39. Cf. Mansi 13: 208D–209C.
40. Nicephoras, *Apol. pro sacris imaginibus* 25 (PG 100, 597A); as quot-

Nicephorus's words here may be compared with those subsequently of Nicetas,[41] acknowledging the leading role that Rome rightly plays in an ecumenical council, though Nicephorus pointedly references Peter and Paul as the sources of Rome's distinction, rather than just Peter.

The support that Rome gave to the defenders of icons throughout the iconoclast controversy led to a greater openness to Roman primacy in the East, but it was a cautious openness—for instance, the Greek version of Pope Hadrian's letter to the Empress Irene that was read at Nicaea II removed the pope's citations of Matt. 16:18ff. and added the name of Paul to that of Peter as founder of the church of Rome[42]—and the recognition that was given to Rome was always in the context of the pentarchy.[43] The idea of the pentarchy actually underwent a significant evolution in the eighth and ninth centuries. Dvornik emphasizes its importance for asserting the rights of the church rather than the emperor with regard to doctrine, and indeed "the infallibility of the Church in matters of doctrine," and he acknowledges also the repeated support given to the church in the East by the pope during the iconoclast crisis.

It was a long struggle that the Eastern Church had to wage, and she was to suffer many defeats which happened, in par-

ed by Dvornik, *Byzantium and the Roman Primacy*, 96 (amended translation).

    41. Cf. above, p. 39.

    42. Cf. Dvornik, *Byzantium and the Roman Primacy*, 96–97.

    43. That is, the idea of the leadership of the church by the five patriarchates: Rome, Constantinople, Alexandria, Antioch, and Jerusalem.

ticular, when a large part of the hierarchy rallied to the side of the emperors who were in heresy. However, they were always able to make a recovery with the aid of the Church of the West, represented by the papacy.[44]

Especially since it is recognized by the Catholic Church as the eighth Ecumenical Council, and because the same council was explicitly cited by Vatican I, it is important to note that it was Constantinople IV (869–70) which particularly developed the idea of the pentarchy. Baanes, representing the emperor, asserted at the council that, led by the five patriarchs, the gates of hell could not prevail against the church (Matt. 16:18).[45] Significantly, it was the other half of the same scriptural verse that was cited by Rome in the *Libellus satisfactionis* that was read at the first session of the council.[46] The passage was subsequently quoted by Vatican I:

The first condition of salvation is to keep the norm of the true faith.... and because it is impossible that those words of our Lord Jesus Christ: "You are Peter and upon this rock I will build my Church" [Matt. 16:18], should not be verified, their truth has been proved in the course of history, for in the apostolic See the Catholic religion has always been kept unsullied, and its teaching kept holy (DH 3066; ND, 319).

Thus, East and West both used Matt. 16:18 but in rather different ways, in support of the pentarchy and papal primacy, respectively. Nevertheless, it is important to note that there was at least a measure of acceptance of the idea

44. Dvornik, *Byzantium and the Roman Primacy*, 103–4.
45. Ibid., 102; cf. de Vries, *Orient et Occident*, 278.
46. Cf. de Vries, *Orient et Occident*, 263.

of the pentarchy in Rome itself, as can be seen from what Anastasius Bibliothecarius wrote in the preface to his translation of the *Acta* of Constantinople IV: "Christ has placed in His body, that is to say, in His Church, a number of patriarchs equal to the number of senses in the human body," and "because, among them, the See of Rome has precedence, it can well be compared to the sense of sight, which is certainly the first of the senses of the body."[47]

Canon 21 of Constantinople IV listed Rome in first place among the "patriarchal sees," followed by Constantinople, Alexandria, Antioch, and Jerusalem (DH 661). The Council of Florence, which like Constantinople IV was also quoted by Vatican I similarly recognized Rome's first place among the patriarchates; it confirmed the canonical order, after the Roman Pontiff, of the "other venerable patriarchs [*ceterorum venerabilium patriarcharum*]," namely the patriarchs of Constantinople, Alexandria, Antioch, and Jerusalem (DH 1308). It was only the teaching of the preceding paragraph, however, regarding the universal primacy of the Roman Pontiff as successor of Peter, vicar of Christ and head of the whole church, that Vatican I cited (DH 3068; cf. 1307). Although, in the aftermath of the Western schism[48] and the council of Constance (1414–18), a rival conciliarist council assembled at Basel (1431–49) and invited the pa-

47. Mansi 16: 7D, as quoted by Dvornik, *Byzantium and the Roman Primacy*, 104; cf. de Vries, *Orient et Occident*, 278. De Vries notes that Baanes's account of the pentarchy did not give Rome precedence (*préséance*); Rome was simply one of the five patriarchal sees (278)

48. The period of two rival popes, in Rome and Avignon, respectively, with eventually a third in Pisa also (1378–1417).

triarch of Constantinople to participate, the patriarch (together with the Eastern emperor and many Eastern bishops) chose to join Pope Eugenius (1431–47) and the ecumenical council he had called at Ferrara-Florence (1438–45), since, within an Eastern pentarchic understanding, an ecumenical council without the bishop of Rome was "as unthinkable ... as it was in the west."[49]

That decision contributed significantly to the defeat of conciliarism, but, as Henn says, the deeper reason for the failure of conciliarism was "the inherent insufficiency of any view which separates or even opposes the ecumenical council and the primacy."[50] In Catholic theology, a separation between an ecumenical council and the pope, that is, a separation between the bishops as a functioning body of leadership in the church and the pope, as posited by conciliarism, is indeed unthinkable. For the same reason, Rahner regards the idea of papal "approbation" of councils as inadequate. "This 'approbation' is, after all, an intrinsic element of the conciliar decree itself, not the adventitious decree of a different authority, conceived as a check on the college, supervening from without as a condition for the validity of the decree, already fully constituted, of the council as a subject apart."[51] As already seen, Vatican II sought to eradicate the possibility of any such separation by its doctrine of collegiality.[52]

49. Chadwick, *East and West*, 263.

50. Henn, "Historical-Theological Synthesis," 247.

51. Rahner, "On the Divine Right of the Episcopate," in Karl Rahner and Joseph Ratzinger, *The Episcopate and the Primacy* (New York: Herder and Herder, 1962), 95.

52. Cf. above, pp. 16, 20, 41–42.

Serving Eucharistic Communion

Ecumenical councils are occasions of the utmost importance in the life of the church: "assembled in an ecumenical council, [the bishops] are, for the universal Church, teachers and judges in matters of faith and morals, whose decisions must be adhered to with the loyal and obedient assent of faith" (LG 25). Such councils express the church's unity at the highest level. However, as the Ravenna document acknowledged: "an Ecumenical Council is not an 'institution' whose frequency can be regulated by canons; it is rather an 'event,' a *kairos* inspired by the Holy Spirit who guides the Church so as to engender within it the institutions which it needs and which respond to its nature" (RD 39). The Catholic Church believes that a universal primacy is such an institution, engendered by the Spirit, corresponding to the church's nature as a Eucharistic communion, and needed by the church to express and serve its unity at the universal level in an *abiding* way. With what can be seen as Eucharistic references to "communion" and "priesthood," Vatican I declared that the universal primacy exists "in order that the episcopate itself might be one and undivided, and that the whole multitude of believers might be preserved in unity of faith and communion by means of a closely united priesthood [*cohaerentes sibi invicem sacerdotes*]" (DH 3051, ND 818).[53]

Jesus died so as "to gather into one the dispersed

53. Cf. above, p. 49.

children of God" (John 11:52), and he prayed to his Father in the Eucharistic context of the Last Supper, on the eve of his death, that his followers might be one "so that the world may believe that you have sent me" (John 17:21). The church's unity is thus essential both to its identity and to its witness in the world. Vatican II stated that Christ filled the church with his Spirit and "provided means adapted to its visible and social union." Jesus is "the author of salvation and the principle of unity and peace," and the church on earth has been established by God as "the visible sacrament of this saving unity" (LG 9). A realistic and effective primacy to manifest and secure that sacramental unity is, accordingly, one of the constitutive gifts of the Lord to his church. Christ perfects the church's "fellowship in unity [*communionem in unitate*]" by the threefold ministry of word, sacrament, and government exercised by "the Apostles and their successors—the bishops with Peter's successor at their head" (UR 2). Given this understanding of the structure of unity established by Christ, anchored in the bishops and centred on the pope, Vatican II stated generally that "our separated brethren ... are not blessed with that unity which Jesus Christ wished to bestow on all those to whom he has given new birth into one body" (UR 3). The unity "which Christ bestowed on his Church from the beginning ... subsists in the Catholic Church" (UR 4).

With regard to the ministry of unity exercised by the bishop of Rome, Pope John Paul II expressed the desire that Catholic and Orthodox pastors and theologians might seek together "the forms in which this ministry may accomplish a service of love recognized by all concerned."[54] In such discussions, it is vital to recall that Vatican II emphasized that the service of love rendered by the universal primate does not involve *government* of the Eastern Churches.

> To remove all shadow of doubt, ... this holy Synod solemnly declares that the Churches of the East, while keeping in mind the necessary unity of the whole Church [*memores necessariae unitatis totius Ecclesiae*], have the power [*facultatem*] to govern themselves according to their own disciplines, since these are better suited to the character of their faithful and better adapted to foster the good of souls. The perfect observance of this traditional principle—which indeed has not always been observed—is a prerequisite for any restoration of union. (UR 16)[55]

In short, it may be said that in Catholic understanding nowadays, what must be sought with regard to the relationship between the pope and the churches of the East is not jurisdiction but communion. The existence and rights of the patriarchates have been canonically recognized, initially by the councils of Nicaea (can. 6), Constantinople I (can. 3), and Chalcedon (can. 28), and subsequently, as seen above, by Constantinople IV (can.

54. *Ut Unum Sint*, n. 95; cf. above, p. 7. Soon afterwards, the CDF similarly stressed that the "ultimate finality" that is proper to the Petrine ministry is "the unity of the Church," and that the actual exercise of that ministry in different places and times will depend on the necessity of the church and will need to be discerned with the help of the Holy Spirit; "Il primato del successore di Pietro nel mistero della chiesa," in *Il Primato del Successore di Pietro*, 493–503, here at 501.

55. Cf. OE 11: "The patriarchal system is the traditional form of government in the Eastern Churches."

21) and the Council of Florence, the latter specifically recognizing the canonical order of the patriarchs "without prejudice to any of their privileges and rights [*salvis privilegiis omnibus et iuribus eorum*]' (DH 1308).[56] Vatican II notably referred to these same councils and canons in its decree on the Catholic Eastern Churches (*Orientalium Ecclesiarum*, OE, 8, note 10),[57] and directed that "the rights and privileges [*iura atque privilegia*]" of the patriarchs of the Eastern Churches "be restored in accordance with the ancient traditions of each church and the decrees of the ecumenical councils" (OE 9).

The Catholic Church thus firmly believes that patriarchal rights must be fully respected, with the sole condition already noted: "while keeping in mind the necessary unity of the whole Church" (UR 16). In *Lumen Gentium*, Vatican II similarly acknowledged the existence "through divine providence" of organic groupings of churches established by the apostles and their successors, "notably the ancient patriarchal Churches," which, "*whilst safeguarding the unity of faith and the unique divine structure [unica divina constitutione] of the universal Church*, have their own discipline, enjoy their own liturgical usage and inherit a theological and spiritual patrimony." Such a multiplicity "*united in a common effort [in unum*

56. Cf. above, p. 71.

57. Note 8 attached to OE 7 also referred to canons 5 and 30 of Lateran IV, which renewed the rights of the patriarchal sees and the traditional *taxis* of Rome, Constantinople, Alexandria, Antioch, and Jerusalem (can.5; with reference to the primacy [*principatum*] of the church of Rome as "*mater universorum Christi fidelium et magistra*," DH 811), and wanted the authority of the Roman Pontiff and the patriarchs to be acknowledged and "the four [*quatuor*] patriarchal sees to be specially honored" (can. 30).

conspirans], shows all the more resplendently the catholicity of the undivided Church" (LG 23, emphasis added). It might be said that the universal primacy willed by the Lord as part of the unique divine structure of the church exists precisely so as to express "the necessary unity of the whole Church" and to serve the "unity of faith" and the "common effort" identified here. Rightly understood, it does not conflict with but rather complements the proper authority of the patriarchs.[58]

With regard to the Catholic Eastern Churches, Vatican II recognized that "patriarchs with their synods are the highest authority for all business of the patriarchate," including the establishment of new eparchies and the appointment of bishops (OE 9). These are thus, patriarchal tasks and the pope himself fulfils them in the Latin Church, even if the papal title of "Patriarch of the West" is no longer used.[59] It is thus clear that the

58. Cf. the teaching of Vatican I, *Pastor Aeternus*, ch.3 (DH 3061), with regard to the relationship between the power of the pope and that of bishops: "this latter power is asserted, confirmed and vindicated by this same supreme and universal shepherd" (DH 3061; ND, 318; above, p. 50). For further discussion of patriarchates and the patriarchal ministry, see George Nedungatt, "The Patriarchal Ministry in the Church of the Third Millennium," *The Jurist* 61 (2001), 1–89; Michael K. Magee, *The Patriarchal Institution in the Church: Ecclesiological Perspectives in the Light of the Second Vatican Council* (Roma: Herder Editrice, 2006); also, Adam A. J. DeVille, *Orthodoxy and the Roman Papacy:* Ut Unum Sint *and the Prospects of East-West Unity* (Notre Dame, Ind.: University of Notre Dame Press, 2011).

59. The communiqué that was issued by the Pontifical Council for Promoting Christian Unity to explain the "suppression" of the title in 2006 from the *Annuario Pontificio*, where it had been used since 1863, said that though it was adopted in 642 by Pope Theodore I, the title's territorial indication was now too vague for effective use. By noting, however, that the pope was listed as first among the patriarchs by the Fourth Council of Constantinople, by the Fourth Lateran Council and by the Council of Flor-

pope already acts differently with regard to the Western and Eastern parts of the Catholic Church itself, in accordance with two distinct codes of canon law for the Church West and East, respectively.[60] While he has additional patriarchal responsibilities in the Latin Church, the pope serves the Catholic Eastern Churches not as patriarch but purely as primate.[61] Vatican II briefly alluded to the prerogatives that pertain to him in the latter role when it referred to his "inalienable right ... to intervene in particular cases [*in singulis casibus*]" (OE 9, amended trans.).[62] The decades since the council show both the rarity of such interventions and the respect with which they are made, and the council made a notable declaration with regard to the provisionality of current arrangements for the "Eastern and Western Catholic Churches": "All these legal arrangements are made in view of present conditions, until such time as the Catholic Church and the separated Eastern Churches unite together in the fullness of communion" (OE 30).

---

ence (cf. above, p. 71 and p. 76, note 57) without the title "Patriarch of the West" being used, the communiqué clearly implied that it was only the title that was being suppressed rather than all notions of a patriarchal role for the pope. In fact, it stated that the bishop of Rome does indeed have a "special relationship" to the Latin Church, and indicated that what the title was referring to, albeit inadequately, was "the particular jurisdiction of the bishop of Rome for the Latin Church" (http://www.vatican.va/roman_curia/pontifical_councils/chrstuni/general-docs/rc_pc_chrstuni_doc_20060322_patriarca-occidente_it.html).

60. Cf. the *Codex Iuris Canonici* (1983) and the *Codex Canonum Ecclesiarum Orientalium* (1990).

61. Cf. above, p. 55.

62. OE 11 also envisaged the establishment of new patriarchates in the East, and said, with references to canons and papal letters of the first millennium: "This is reserved to an ecumenical council or to the Roman Pontiff."

With regard to the Western, or Latin, Church, Vatican II indicated that regional or national episcopal conferences have some similarities to Eastern patriarchates in that they "contribute in many and fruitful ways to the concrete realisation of the collegial spirit" (LG 23). It encouraged the formation of episcopal conferences "in all parts of the world," and expressed the hope that synods and councils at various levels "may flourish with renewed vigor" (CD 36–37). Of particular significance was the establishment by Pope Paul VI in 1965 of the Synod of Bishops, "representative of the whole Catholic episcopate," to assist the pope and "bear testimony to the participation of all the bishops in hierarchical communion in the care of the universal Church" (CD 5).[63] So far, more than a dozen ordinary general assemblies of the Synod have been held at regular intervals, and many special assemblies dedicated to particular continents or regions, also. This renewed synodal activity, together with the regular life of episcopal conferences now found in all parts of the Catholic Church in the West, has been a marked feature of the Catholic Church since Vatican II. Nevertheless, the role of the Synod of Bishops is limited: "it advises the pope; it is not a small-scale Council, and it is not a collegial organ of leadership for the universal Church."[64]

It was noted above that Vatican II deliberately avoided the medieval *per Petrum* notion, which fostered the idea of Rome as "mother of all churches" and of the pope's con-

63. Cf. above, p. 20–21.
64. Joseph Ratzinger, *Church, Ecumenism and Politics* (Slough: St Paul, 1988), 46.

sequent jurisdiction over all churches,[65] *Lumen Gentium* gave further evidence of this changed stance when it recognized the "ancient patriarchal Churches" as "mothers in the faith" which have given birth to "daughter-Churches" and remain linked to them "by bonds of a more intimate charity in what pertains to the sacramental life and in a mutual respect for rights and obligations [*in mutua iurium et officiorum reverentia*]" (LG 23). Cardinal Ratzinger gave a clear statement of the Catholic Church's present understanding of the idea of "Mother Church," in which the former idea of Rome as mother of all churches is conspicuously absent:

[T]he Church of Rome is the Mother Church of the Churches in Italy, but not of course the Mother Church of all the others. Jerusalem is the Mother Church of many Churches; Antioch and Constantinople are Mother Churches. Yet this "motherhood" can be only an image of the real "Mother Church"— the "Jerusalem above" that Paul talks about (Gal. 4:26), of which the Fathers speak so movingly.[66]

The *Note on the Expression «Sister Churches»* that was issued by the CDF in 2000 may also be heeded in this regard, because, while not approving the idea that the Catholic Church and the Orthodox Church themselves are sisters, it readily endorsed the usage according to which "the particular Church of Rome can ... be called the *sister* of all other particular Churches," both Catholic

---

65. Cf. above, pp. 37–40.
66. "Exchange of Letters between Metropolitan Damaskinos and Cardinal Joseph Ratzinger," in Joseph Ratzinger, *Pilgrim Fellowship of Faith* (San Francisco: Ignatius, 2005), 217–41, here at 238–39.

and Orthodox particular churches being understood.[67]

The idea of Rome as mother, "source and origin"[68] of all churches, and of the pope correspondingly having jurisdiction over all churches is characteristic of the second millennium, not the first.[69] The ecclesiology of communion, characteristic of the first millennium and based on the Eucharist, was renewed by Vatican II,[70] and that is what provides the context within which the Catholic Church is currently seeking full communion once again with the Orthodox Church. The Catholic Church believes that the universal primacy exists *iure divino* as the episcopate itself exists *iure divino* (DH 3115),[71] and that the purpose of the universal primacy is that "the episcopate itself might be one and undivided, and that the whole multitude of believers might be preserved in unity of faith and communion by means of a closely united priesthood" (DH 3051, ND 818).[72] The "unique divine structure of the universal Church" which must be safeguarded (LG 23) is the communion which the church enjoys by its participation in the trinitarian life of God (cf. LG 4, UR 2, GS 24), such that the church on earth is a sacrament of "saving unity" and communion (LG 1,

---

67. CDF, *Note on the Expression «Sister Churches»* (2000), 11. For discussion of the idea of sister churches, see the articles by Emmanuel Lanne, "Églises unis ou églises soeurs: Un choix ineluctable," *Irénikon* 48 (1975), 322–42; "Églises-soeurs: Implications ecclésiologiques du *Tomos Agapis*," *Istina* 25 (1975), 47–74.

68. Henn, "Historical-Theological Synthesis," 231.

69. Cf. above, pp. 27, 35, 38, 53–54.

70. Cf. above, pp. 7–8, 10, 16–17, 22–23, 48–49.

71. Cf. above, p. 48.

72. Cf. above, pp. 49, 73.

9). The college of bishops and the pope are essential to that "unique divine structure"—or, better, the college of bishops headed by the pope *is* essential to that structure—as a corporate sign and servant of the communion life of the church as a whole.[73] Rome is not mother and source of all the churches in a *per Petrum* configuration; rather it is the head or first of the churches, and the bishop of Rome is the head or first of the bishops (LG 22), in a communional configuration.[74]

As the head or first of the bishops, the bishop of Rome has specific prerogatives, which have readily been recognized in the East.[75] As seen above, Vatican II particularly drew attention to the role of the Roman see and its bishop in moderating disagreements between the churches in faith and discipline (UR 14) and in recognizing and participating in ecumenical councils (LG 25). Henn notes that the period since Vatican II has seen a "shift away from the language of jurisdiction toward that of communion" and is correspondingly characterized by "a different perspective for understanding the relation between primacy and episcopacy than that which dominated the West since the time of Gregory VII."[76] Vatican II evoked the perspective of the first millennium, the perspective for Catholic-Orthodox reconciliation, when it referred

73. Cf. above, p. 4, note 7.

74. Cf. above, p. 3.

75. Cf. Nicetas (above, pp. 38–40) and Phidas (pp. 55–56). Battifol's reference to the bishops of major Eastern sees announcing their election to the bishop of Rome in order to obtain his communion is also relevant here (above, p. 53).

76. Henn, "Historical-Theological synthesis," 271.

to "the very ancient discipline whereby the bishops installed throughout the whole world lived in communion with one another and with the Roman Pontiff in a bond of unity, charity, and peace" (LG 22). Encompassing but also beyond merely action in specific cases of dispute and involvement in the extraordinary occasions of ecumenical councils, it may be said that the universal primacy exists lastingly and fundamentally in order to serve the harmony of the church in unity, charity, and peace that comes from its regular Eucharistic life.

4

CONCLUSION

Vatican II stated: "Nothing more should be demanded of separated Eastern Christians who come to Catholic unity under the influence of the grace of the Holy Spirit than what the simple profession of the Catholic faith requires" (OE 25). Because the Catholic Church believes that a universal primacy exists *iure divino*, this stipulation of what the Catholic faith requires is understood to include an acceptance of universal primacy. With regard to the form of that primacy, however, Joseph Ratzinger commented at Graz in 1976 that the form the primacy has taken in the nineteenth and twentieth centuries is not the only possible form, and therefore that it is not "binding on all Christians." He famously added: "Rome must not require more from the East with respect to the doctrine of the primacy than had been formulated and was lived in the first millennium."[1] He recalled that Patriarch Athenagoras had greeted Pope Paul VI on the latter's visit to Constantinople on July 25, 1967, as "successor of Peter," "the first in honor among us," and "the

1. Joseph Ratzinger, *Principles of Catholic Theology: Building Stones for a Fundamental Theology* (San Francisco: Ignatius Press, 1987), 198–99.

one who presides in charity,"[2] and he observed that this was "the essential content of the doctrine of primacy as it was known in the first millennium." "Rome need not ask for more,"[3] he firmly concluded.

Later in the same address, Ratzinger concentrated on the second and third of the phrases used by Patriarch Athenagoras and asked whether "this archaic confession, which has nothing to do with the 'primacy of jurisdiction' but confesses a primacy of 'honor' (τιμή) and *agape*, might not be recognized as a formula that adequately reflects the position Rome occupies in the Church."[4] He thus translated the general idea that what was confessed in the first millennium might suffice for today into a brief and memorable concrete form, leaving aside the issue of *jurisdiction* and highlighting expressions from the First Council of Constantinople and Ignatius of Antioch, respectively. The first of these refers, as we have seen, to the *honor of primacy*,[5] and the second is *Eucharistic*.[6]

It is notable that Ratzinger did not insist on the first phrase that Patriarch Athenagoras used—"successor of Peter." As seen above, this phrase can be understood in various ways,[7] and, while the bishops of Rome from the fourth century onwards tended to emphasize their con-

2. The three titles are quoted here from E. J. Storman, ed., *Towards the Healing of Schism: The Sees of Rome and Constantinople. Public Statements and Correspondence between the Holy See and the Ecumenical Patriarchate 1958–1984* (New York/Mahwah, N. J.: Paulist Press, 1987), 159 (final phrase amended).

3. Ratzinger, *Principles of Catholic Theology*, 199.

4. Ibid., 217.   5. Cf. above, p. 55.

6. Cf. above, p. 27.   7. Cf. above, p. 54.

nection with Peter in particular, as successor, heir, or vicar,[8] the East never accepted this idea[9] and preferred the idea that the bishop of Rome was simply bishop of the church founded by both Peter and Paul.[10] Patriarch Athenagoras did use the phrase "successor of Peter" but immediately made mention of Paul, too, as patron saint of the pope he was greeting: "Welcome then, holy brother and successor of Peter, one with Paul in name and manner, messenger of love, unity, and peace."[11]

What is perhaps most striking is that the expression, "messenger of love, unity, and peace," echoes Vatican II's description of the communion that united the bishops of the church with one another and with the bishop of Rome in the early centuries as "a bond of unity, charity, and peace" (LG 22).[12] Bearing in mind that love, unity, and peace are all fruits of the one Eucharist that Catholics and Orthodox both celebrate, it would seem that "messenger of love, unity, and peace" might be a promising way for Catholics and Orthodox together to describe a universal primate who sums up in himself what all the bishops are, and who serves their Eucharistic communion.

We may finally observe that the Eucharistic resonance of the word *agape* (love) in Ignatius's greeting to

8. Cf. above, pp. 23–24, 54.

9. Cf. above, p. 54.

10. Cf. above, p. 69. It may be noted in this regard that Ignatius of Antioch in his letter to the Romans makes only one reference to Peter and one to Paul, recalling them together in the phrase: "I am not issuing orders to you, as though I were a Peter or a Paul" (*Letter to the Romans*, 4).

11. Storman, *Towards the Healing of Schism*, 159.

12. Cf. above, p. 83.

the church of Rome means that Pope John Paul's phrase "a service of love,"[13] used to express the primatial ministry of the bishop of Rome, can itself be interpreted as meaning a service to the Eucharist, and to the ecclesial communion that flows from it. It was in terms of just such a service that Joseph Ratzinger, as Pope Benedict XVI, described the ministry to which he himself had been called, and it seems highly fitting to close with his words:

The Eucharist is the *Sacramentum caritatis Christi*, through which Christ continues to draw us all to himself, as he did when raised up on the Cross (cf. John 12:32). Therefore, to "preside in charity" is to draw men and women into a eucharistic embrace—the embrace of Christ—which surpasses every barrier and every division, creating communion from all manner of differences. The Petrine ministry is therefore a primacy of love in the eucharistic sense, that is to say solicitude for the universal communion of the Church in Christ. And the Eucharist is the shape and the measure of this communion, a guarantee that it will remain faithful to the criterion of the tradition of the faith.[14]

13. Cf. above, p. 7.
14. Pope Benedict XVI, Homily at the Eucharistic Concelebration with the New Cardinals, Sunday, February 19, 2012 (http://www.vatican.va/holy_father/benedict_xvi/homilies/2012/documents/hf_ben-xvi_hom_20120219_nuovi-cardinali_en.html).

Appendix

ECUMENICAL COUNCILS

325	(First) Council of Nicaea
381	(First) Council of Constantinople
431	Council of Ephesus
451	Council of Chalcedon
553	Second Council of Constantinople (Constantinople II)
680–81	Third Council of Constantinople (Constantinople III)
787	Second Council of Nicaea (Nicaea II)

The seven councils listed above are recognized by both Catholics and Orthodox as ecumenical. Especially in the Christian East, they are sometimes known simply by their numbering, that is, the first ecumenical council, the second ecumenical council, etc., numbering being intrinsic to the recognition of a council as ecumenical (cf. above, p. 68). Orthodox generally regard the Second Council of Nicaea as the seventh and last ecumenical council, so far, at least.

869–70 Fourth Council of Constantinople (Constantinople IV)

Constantinople IV is recognized as ecumenical by the Catholic Church. However, its status is somewhat dubious. A significant body of opinion, both Catholic and Orthodox, would prefer to designate the later council of 879–80, also held in Constantinople, as the eighth ecumenical council (cf. above, p. 63, note 28).

The Catholic Church considers the following councils, held in the West since the schism of 1054, also as ecumenical:

1123	First Lateran Council (Lateran I)
1139	Second Lateran Council (Lateran II)
1179	Third Lateran Council (Lateran III)
1215	Fourth Lateran Council (Lateran IV)
1245	First Council of Lyons (Lyons I)
1274	Second Council of Lyons (Lyons II)
1311–12	Council of Vienne
1414–18	Council of Constance
1438–45	Council of Florence
1545–63	Council of Trent
1869–70	First Vatican Council (Vatican I)
1962–65	Second Vatican Council (Vatican II)

BIBLIOGRAPHY

Afanassieff, N. "Una Sancta." *Irenikon* 36 (1963): 436–75. [Nicolas
    Afanasiev. "Una Sancta." In *Tradition Alive,* edited by Michael
    Plekon, 3–30. Lanham, Md.: Rowman and Littlefield, 2003.]
Battifol, Pierre. *Cathedra Petri.* Paris: Cerf, 1938.
Benedict XVI, Pope. Apostolic Exhortation. *Sacramentum Caritatis,*
    2007.
————. *Luce del mondo.* Vatican City: Libreria Editrice Vaticana,
    2010. [Michael J. Miller and Adrian J. Walker, trans. *The Light
    of the World: A Conversation with Peter Seewald.* San Francisco:
    Ignatius Press, 2010.]
Benson, Robert L. "Plenitudo potestatis: Evolution of a formula
    from Gregory IV to Gratian." *Studia Gratiana* 14 (1967): 193–207.
Chadwick, Henry. *East and West: The Making of a Rift in the Church.*
    Oxford: Oxford University Press, 2003.
Chapman, Dom John. *Studies on the Early Papacy.* London: Sheed &
    Ward, 1928.
Congar, Yves. "De la communion des églises à une ecclésiologie de
    l'Église universelle." In *L'Épiscopat et l'Église universelle,* edited by
    Y. Congar and B. D. Dupuy, 227–60. Paris: Cerf, 1964.
————. "L' «Ecclesia» ou communauté chrétienne, sujet intégral
    de l'action liturgique." In. *La Liturgie après Vatican II,* edited by
    J.-P. Jossua and Y. Congar, 241–82. Paris: Cerf, 1967.
————. *Diversités et communion.* Paris: Cerf, 1982. [*Diversity and
    Communion,* translated by John Bowden. London: SCM, 1984.]
————. "A Last Look at the Council." In *Vatican II by Those Who
    Were There,* edited by Alberic Stacpoole, 337–58. London: Geof-
    frey Chapman, 1986.

———. *Église et Papauté.* Paris: Cerf, 1994.

Congregation for the Doctrine of the Faith. *Mysterium Fidei.* Declaration in Defense of the Catholic Doctrine on the Church against Some Present-Day Errors. 1973.

———. *Communionis Notio.* Letter to the Bishops of the Catholic Church on Some Aspects of the Church Understood as Communion. 1992.

———. "Il primato del successore di Pietro nel mistero della chiesa." In *Il Primato del Successore di Pietro: Atti del simposio teologico. Roma, dicembre 1996,* 493–503. Città del Vaticano: Libreria Editrice Vaticana. 1998.

———. *Note on the Expression «Sister Churches».* 2000.

Daley, Brian E. "Position and Patronage in the Early Church: The Original Meaning of 'Primacy of Honour.'" In *Journal of Theological Studies* 44 (1993): 529–53.

DeVille, Adam A. J. *Orthodoxy and the Roman Papacy: Ut Unum Sint and the Prospects of East-West Unity.* Notre Dame, Ind.: University of Notre Dame Press, 2011.

Duffy, Eamon. *Saints and Sinners: A History of the Popes.* 3rd ed. New Haven and London: Yale University Press, 2006.

Dupuy, Bernard. "Les appels de l'Orient à Rome du concile de Nicée au concile de Chalcédoine." *Istina* 32 (1987): 361–77.

Dvornik, Francis. *Byzantium and the Roman Primacy.* New York: Fordham University Press, 1966.

Empie, Paul C., and Murphy, T. Austin, eds. *Papal Primacy and the Universal Church.* Minneapolis: Augsburg Publishing House, 1974.

Fortescue, Adrian. "Holy Synod." *The Catholic Encyclopedia,* vol. 7, 428–32. New York: The Gilmary Society, 1913.

Henn, William. "Historical-Theological Synthesis of the Relation between Primacy and Episcopacy during the Second Millennium." In *Il Primato del Successore di Pietro: Atti del simposio teologico. Roma, dicembre 1996,* 222–73. Città del Vaticano: Libreria Editrice Vaticana, 1998.

———. *The Honor of My Brothers: A Short History of the Relations between the Pope and the Bishops.* New York: Crossroad, 2000.

John Paul II, Pope. *Ut Unum Sint.* Encyclical Letter. (1995).

———. *Ecclesia de Eucharistia.* Encyclical Letter. (2003).

Joint International Commission for Theological Dialogue between
the Roman Catholic Church and the Orthodox Church. *The
Mystery of the Church and of the Eucharist in the Light of the Mystery
of the Holy Trinity.* 1982. (The Munich document.)

————. *Ecclesiological and Canonical Consequences of the Sacramental Nature of the Church: Ecclesial Communion, Conciliarity and
Authority.* 2007. (The Ravenna document.)

Kasper, Walter Cardinal. *Sakrament der Einheit. Eucharistie und
Kirche.* Freiburg: Herder, 2004. [*Sacrament of Unity: The Eucharist
and the Church*, translated by Brian McNeil. New York: Crossroad, 2004.]

————. "Introduction to the Theme and Catholic Hermeneutics
of the Dogmas of the First Vatican Council." In *The Petrine
Ministry: Catholics and Orthodox in Dialogue,* edited by Walter
Cardinal Kasper, 7–23. New York/Mahwah N. J.: The Newman
Press, 2006.

Lanne, Emmanuel. "Églises-soeurs: Implications ecclésiologiques
du *Tomos Agapis.*" *Istina* 25 (1975): 47–74.

————. "Églises unis ou églises soeurs: Un choix inéluctable."
Irénikon 48 (1975): 322–42.

Legrand, Hervé. "Pour une approche procédurale de la primauté
romaine." *Istina* 53 (2008): 23–46.

Louth, Andrew. *Greek East and Latin West: The Church AD 681–1071.*
The Church in History 3. Crestwood, N.Y.: St Vladimir's Seminary Press, 2007.

de Lubac, Henri. *Catholicisme.* Paris: Cerf, 1938. [*Catholicism*, translated by Lancelot C. Sheppard and Sister Elizabeth Englund,
OCD. San Francisco: Ignatius Press, 1988.]

————. *Corpus Mysticum: L'eucharistie et L'Église au moyen age.* 2nd
ed. Paris: Aubier 1949. [*Corpus Mysticum: The Eucharist and the
Church in the Middle Ages,* translated by Gemma Simmonds, CJ,
with Richard Price. London: SCM, 2006.]

————. *Méditation sur l'Église.* 2nd ed. Paris: Aubier, 1953. [*The
Splendor of the Church,* translated by Michael Mason. San Francisco: Ignatius Press, 1986.]

————. *Les églises particulières dans l'Église universelle.* Paris: Aubier,
1971. [*The Motherhood of the Church,* translated by Sr. Sergia
Englund, OCD. San Francisco: Ignatius Press, 1982.]

McPartlan, Paul. "Eucharistic Ecclesiology." *One in Christ* 22 (1986): 314–31.

———. *Sacrament of Salvation: An Introduction to Eucharistic Ecclesiology.* Edinburgh: T & T Clark, 1995.

———. *The Eucharist Makes the Church: Henri de Lubac and John Zizioulas in Dialogue.* 2nd ed. Fairfax, Va.: Eastern Christian Publications, 2006.

———. "*Ressourcement*, Vatican II, and Eucharistic Ecclesiology." In Ressourcement: *A Movement for Renewal in Twentieth-Century Catholic Theology,* edited by Gabriel Flynn and Paul D. Murray, 392–404. Oxford: Oxford University Press, 2012.

Magee, Michael K. *The Patriarchal Institution in the Church: Ecclesiological Perspectives in the Light of the Second Vatican Council.* Roma: Herder Editrice, 2006.

Minnerath, Roland. "La tradition de la primauté pétrinienne au premier millénaire." In *Il Primato del Successore di Pietro: Atti del simposio teologico. Roma, dicembre 1996,* 117–45. Città del Vaticano: Libreria Editrice Vaticana, 1998.

Mondin, Battista. *Le nuove ecclesiologie.* Roma: Edizioni Paoline, 1980.

Nedungatt, George. "The Patriarchal Ministry in the Church of the Third Millennium." *The Jurist* 61 (2001): 1–89.

Phidas, Vlassios. "Papal Primacy and Patriarchal Pentarchy in the Orthodox Tradition." In *The Petrine Ministry: Catholics and Orthodox in Dialogue,* edited by Walter Cardinal Kasper, 65–82. New York/Mahwah N. J.: The Newman Press, 2006.

Pottmeyer, Hermann J. *Towards a Papacy in Communion: Perspectives from Vatican Councils I & II.* New York: Herder and Herder, 1998.

Rahner, Karl. "On the Divine Right of the Episcopacy " In *The Episcopate and the Primacy,* by Karl Rahner and Joseph Ratzinger, 64–135. New York: Herder and Herder, 1962.

Rahner, Karl, and Joseph Ratzinger. *Episkopat und Primat.* Freiburg: Herder, 1961. [*The Episcopate and the Primacy,* translated by Kenneth Barker and others. New York: Herder and Herder, 1962.]

Ratzinger, Joseph. "The Pastoral Implications of Episcopal Collegiality." *Concilium* 1, no.1 (1965): 20–34.

———. *Theologische Prinzipienlehre: Bausteine zur Fundamental-theologie*. Munich: Wewel Verlag, 1986. [*Principles of Catholic Theology: Building Stones for a Fundamental Theology,* translated by Mary Frances McCarthy. San Francisco: Ignatius, 1987].

———. *Kirche, Ökumene und Politik*. Einsiedeln: Johannes-Verlag, 1987. [*Church, Ecumenism and Politics,* translated by Robert Nowell, also Frideswide Sandeman. Slough, U.K.: St Paul Publications, 1988.]

———. *Zur Gemeinschaft gerufen: Kirche heute verstehen*. 2nd ed. Freiburg im Breisgau: Herder, 1991. [*Called to Communion: Understanding the Church Today,* translated by Adrian Walker. San Francisco: Ignatius Press, 1996.]

———. *Weg Gemeinschaft des Glaubens: Kirche als Communio*. Augsburg: Sankt Ulrich Verlag, 2002. [*Pilgrim Fellowship of Faith: The Church as Communion,* translated by Henry Taylor. San Francisco: Ignatius Press, 2005.]

Rivière, Jean. "In partem sollicitudinis: Évolution d'une formule pontificale." *Revue des sciences religieuses* 5 (1925): 210–31.

Robinson, I. S. "Church and Papacy." In *The Cambridge History of Medieval Political Thought c. 350–c.1450,* edited by J. H. Burns, 252–305. Cambridge: Cambridge University Press, 1988.

Rush, Ormond. *The Eyes of Faith: The Sense of the Faithful and the Church's Reception of Revelation*. Washington, D.C.: The Catholic University of America Press, 2009.

Simonetti, Manlio. *La crisi ariana nel IV secolo*. Roma: Institutum Patristicum «Augustinianum», 1975.

Stevenson, J. *Creeds, Councils and Controversies: Documents Illustrating the History of the Church, AD 337–461*. London: SPCK, 1987.

Storman, E. J., ed. *Towards the Healing of Schism: The Sees of Rome and Constantinople. Public Statements and Correspondence between the Holy See and the Ecumenical Patriarchate 1958–1984*. New York/Mahwah, N. J.: Paulist Press, 1987.

Tillard, J. M. R. "Sensus Fidelium." *One in Christ* 11 (1975): 2–29.

———. *L'évêque de Rome*. Paris: Cerf, 1982. [*The Bishop of Rome,* translated by John de Satgé. London: SPCK, 1983.]

———. *Chair de l'Église, chair du Christ: Aux sources de l'ecclésiologie de communion*. Paris: Cerf, 1992. [*Flesh of the Church, Flesh of Christ: At* the *Source of the Ecclesiology of Communion*, translated by Madeleine Beaumont. Collegeville, Minn.: Liturgical Press, 2001.]

Ullmann, Walter. "Leo I and the Theme of Papal Primacy." *Journal of Theological Studies* 11 (1960): 25–51.

Vatican Council I. *Pastor Aeternus.* First Dogmatic Constitution on the Church. 1870.

Vatican Council II. *Sacrosanctum Concilium.* Constitution on the Sacred Liturgy. 1963.

———. *Lumen Gentium.* Dogmatic Constitution on the Church. 1964.

———. *Orientalium Ecclesiarum.* Decree on the Catholic Eastern Churches. 1964.

———. *Unitatis Redintegratio.* Decree on Ecumenism. 1964.

———. *Christus Dominus.* Decree on the Pastoral Office of Bishops in the Church. 1965.

———. *Dei Verbum.* Dogmatic Constitution on Divine Revelation. 1965.

———. *Gaudium et Spes.* Pastoral Constitution on the Church. 1965.

de Vries, W. *Orient et Occident: Les structures ecclésiales vues dans l'histoire des sept premiers conciles oecuméniques.* Paris: Cerf, 1974.

Watt, John A. *The Theory of Papal Monarchy in the Thirteenth Century: The Contribution of the Canonists.* London: Burns & Oates, 1965.

Zizioulas, John. *Being as Communion: Studies in Personhood and the Church.* London: Darton, Longman and Todd, 1985.

———. *Eucharist, Bishop, Church: The Unity of the Church in the Divine Eucharist and in the Bishop during the First Three Centuries*, translated by Elizabeth Theokritoff. Brookline, Mass.: Holy Cross Orthodox Press, 2001.

———. *Communion and Otherness: Further Studies in Personhood and the Church*, edited by Paul McPartlan. London: T & T Clark, 2006.

———. *The Eucharistic Communion and the World*, edited by Luke Ben Tallon. London: T & T Clark, 2011.

INDEX

A Service of Love: Papal Primacy, the Eucharist, and Church Unity was designed and typeset in Maiola by Kachergis Book Design of Pittsboro, North Carolina. It was printed on 60-pound Natures Book Recycled and bound by McNaughton & Gunn of Saline, Michigan.